An Anthology of Poetry by Women

Also available from Cassell:

Carol Fox: *At the Very Edge of the Forest: The Influence of Literature on Storytelling by Children*

Morag Styles, Eve Bearne and Victor Watson (editors): *After Alice: Exploring Children's Literature*

Morag Styles, Eve Bearne and Victor Watson (editors): *The Prose and the Passion: Children and Their Reading*

An Anthology of Poetry by Women

TRACING THE TRADITION

LINDA HALL

CASSELL

Cassell

Villiers House	387 Park Avenue South
41/47 Strand	New York
London	NY 10016-8810
WC2N 5JE	

Arrangement and commentary © Linda Hall 1994

First published 1994

British Library Cataloguing-in-Publication Data
A catalogue record for this book is available from the British Library.

ISBN 0-304-32415-9 (hardback)
0-304-32434-5 (paperback)

Typeset by Litho Link Ltd, Welshpool, Powys, Wales
Printed and bound in Great Britain by Biddles Ltd, Guildford and King's Lynn

Contents

Introduction   1

LOVE AND PASSION

Introduction   3

From Sonnets from the Portuguese (I, XX and XXXII)   6
    ELIZABETH BARRETT BROWNING

On Monsieur's Departure   8
    ELIZABETH I

Sonnets XLII and XXXIII   9
    ELEANOR FARJEON

Cousin Kate   10
    CHRISTINA ROSSETTI

'Fair, Do You Not See . . .'   11
    SYLVIA TOWNSEND WARNER

An Answer to a Love Letter   12
    LADY MARY WORTLEY MONTAGU

The Lady's Yes   13
    ELIZABETH BARRETT BROWNING

Remembrance   14
    EMILY BRONTË

'In June and Gentle Oven'   15
    ANNE WILKINSON

Monna Innominata (Sonnets II, VII and XI)   16
    CHRISTINA ROSSETTI

Song: A Thousand Martyrs I Have Made   18
    APHRA BEHN

Sonnet XLI   18
    EDNA ST VINCENT MILLAY

I Love You with My Life 19
MICHAEL FIELD

Drawing You, Heavy with Sleep 19
SYLVIA TOWNSEND WARNER

MOTHERHOOD

Introduction 20

Before the Birth of One of Her Children 22
ANNE BRADSTREET

Calliope in the Labour Ward 22
ELAINE FEINSTEIN

Maternal Grief 23
KATHLEEN RAINE

Maternity 24
ALICE MEYNELL

Orinda upon Little Hector Philips 24
KATHERINE PHILIPS

Mother and Poet 25
ELIZABETH BARRETT BROWNING

Parentage 28
ALICE MEYNELL

The Scholar 29
FRANCES CORNFORD

Sonnet XXVIII 29
ELEANOR FARJEON

Sonnet XII 30
ELINOR WYLIE

The Modern Mother 30
ALICE MEYNELL

Sick Boy 31
ANNE RIDLER

Child Waking 31
E. J. SCOVELL

The First Year 32
E. J. SCOVELL

RELATIONS BETWEEN THE SEXES

Introduction 34

The Wife's Lament 37
Translated by KEMP MALONE

The Homecoming 39
ANNA WICKHAM

To the Ladies 40
LADY MARY CHUDLEIGH

The Man with a Hammer 40
ANNA WICKHAM

The Emulation 41
SARAH FYGE EGERTON

A Clever Woman 42
MARY ELIZABETH COLERIDGE

The Witch 42
ADELAIDE CRAPSEY

The Farmer's Bride 43
CHARLOTTE MEW

A Man's Requirements 44
ELIZABETH BARRETT BROWNING

Maude Clare 46
CHRISTINA ROSSETTI

The Contract 47
EMILY DICKINSON

From Brother and Sister Sonnets (1, 5 and 9) 48
GEORGE ELIOT

Woman's Song 50
SYLVIA TOWNSEND WARNER

Marriage and Death 51
E. J. SCOVELL

An April Epithalamium   51
ANNE STEVENSON

FAITH AND RELIGION

Introduction   53

Psalms lxxi and lxxii   55
MARY HERBERT

From Contemplations   55
ANNE BRADSTREET

The Soul's Home   56
ANNE COLLINS

In Sleep   57
ALICE MEYNELL

Uphill   57
CHRISTINA ROSSETTI

No Coward Soul Is Mine   58
EMILY BRONTË

To a Friend with a Religious Vocation   59
ELIZABETH JENNINGS

Now As Then   60
ANNE RIDLER

Early One Morning . . .   60
SYLVIA TOWNSEND WARNER

Those dying then   61
EMILY DICKINSON

Faith is a fine invention   61
EMILY DICKINSON

Mother, among the Dustbins   62
STEVIE SMITH

Sonnet LXVIII   63
EDNA ST VINCENT MILLAY

Innocent Landscape   63
ELINOR WYLIE

Because I could not stop for Death 64
 EMILY DICKINSON

Hymn for Holy Deconsecration 65
 SYLVIA TOWNSEND WARNER

DEATH

Introduction 66

Nature's Cook 69
 MARGARET CAVENDISH, DUCHESS OF NEWCASTLE

The Mummy Invokes His Soul 70
 MICHAEL FIELD

I heard a fly buzz when I died 70
 EMILY DICKINSON

Rembrandt's Late Self-Portraits 71
 ELIZABETH JENNINGS

Castle Wood 71
 EMILY BRONTË

First Death in Nova Scotia 72
 ELIZABETH BISHOP

Tropical Death 74
 GRACE NICHOLS

Memorial to D.C. (Vassar College, 1918) 75
 EDNA ST VINCENT MILLAY

A Dirge 76
 CHRISTINA ROSSETTI

Abbey Tomb 77
 PATRICIA BEER

Drowning is not so pitiful 78
 EMILY DICKINSON

Nothing Is Lost 78
 ANNE RIDLER

Remember 79
 CHRISTINA ROSSETTI

WAR

Introduction   80

Battle Hymn of the Republic   83
JULIA WARD HOWE

The Beau Ideal   84
JESSIE POPE

I Sit and Sew   85
ALICE DUNBAR NELSON

Summer in England, 1914   86
ALICE MEYNELL

From a Letter to America on a Visit to Sussex: Spring 1942   87
FRANCES CORNFORD

From Why Ask to Know the Date – the Clime?   87
EMILY BRONTË

Easter Monday: In Memoriam E.T.   88
ELEANOR FARJEON

A War Film   89
TERESA HOOLEY

Missing, Presumed Killed   90
PAMELA HOLMES

A Son   90
LILIAN BOWES LYON

Evacuee   91
EDITH PICKTHALL

The Evacuees   91
FREDA LAUGHTON

POLITICS AND SOCIAL PROTEST

Introduction   92

From The Cry of the Children   95
ELIZABETH BARRETT BROWNING

On Seeing an Officer's Widow Distracted . . .   99
MARY BARBER

Kitchenette Building 100
GWENDOLYN BROOKS

The Choosing 100
LIZ LOCHHEAD

A Father of Women 102
ALICE MEYNELL

The Woman's Labour, an Epistle 103
MARY COLLIER

From Insec' Lesson 110
VALERIE BLOOM

The Two Boys 111
MARY LAMB

From A Royal Princess 111
CHRISTINA ROSSETTI

When the Night and Morning Meet 115
DORA GREENWELL

From A Minor Prophet 116
GEORGE ELIOT

The Hunting *of the Hare* 120
MARGARET CAVENDISH, DUCHESS OF NEWCASTLE

Lucky 123
GERDA MAYER

LITERATURE AND ART

Introduction 125
'Soothing and Awful' 128
U. A. FANTHORPE

A Performance of Henry V at Stratford-upon-Avon 129
ELIZABETH JENNINGS

Bronze Trumpets and Sea Water – On Turning Latin
into English 130
ELINOR WYLIE

From The Land   130
  VITA SACKVILLE-WEST

Aunt Jennifer's Tigers   132
  ADRIENNE RICH

Melinda on an Insippid Beauty   132
  ANNE FINCH

In an Artist's Studio   133
  CHRISTINA ROSSETTI

'O May I Join the Choir Invisible'   133
  GEORGE ELIOT

The White Women   134
  MARY ELIZABETH COLERIDGE

Songless   136
  ALICE WALKER

Silent Is the House   137
  EMILY BRONTË

A Policeman's Lot   139
  WENDY COPE

I think I was enchanted   140
  EMILY DICKINSON

The Season's Lovers   141
  MIRIAM WADDINGTON

SEPARATION AND SUFFERING

Introduction   143

Eadwacer   145
  Translated by KEMP MALONE

To Mrs M.A. upon Absence   146
  KATHERINE PHILIPS

Patterns   147
  AMY LOWELL

The Other Side of a Mirror   150
  MARY ELIZABETH COLERIDGE

Written in Her French Psalter 151
ELIZABETH I

I Am the Only Being 151
EMILY BRONTË

Lineage 152
MARGARET WALKER

From Brother and Sister Sonnets (11) 152
GEORGE ELIOT

Solitude 153
ELLA WHEELER WILCOX

A Better Resurrection 154
CHRISTINA ROSSETTI

Paralytic 154
SYLVIA PLATH

Address to My Soul 156
ELINOR WYLIE

Floating Island at Hawkshead 157
DOROTHY WORDSWORTH

THE NATURAL WORLD

Introduction 158

From Wild Peaches 160
ELINOR WYLIE

Noon 161
MICHAEL FIELD

Thoughts on My Sick-bed 162
DOROTHY WORDSWORTH

All Things Bright and Beautiful 164
MRS C. F. ALEXANDER

The Trees Are Down 164
CHARLOTTE MEW

A narrow fellow in the grass 166
EMILY DICKINSON

For a Five-Year-Old   167
FLEUR ADCOCK

Cold-blooded Creatures   167
ELINOR WYLIE

Whiteness I Remember   168
SYLVIA PLATH

Pain for a Daughter   169
ANNE SEXTON

Another Spring   171
CHRISTINA ROSSETTI

Autumn Chant   172
EDNA ST VINCENT MILLAY

From The Land   172
VITA SACKVILLE-WEST

Where I Come From   173
ELIZABETH BREWSTER

Index of Authors   174
Index of First Lines   175
Acknowledgements   178

Introduction

T HE poems in this anthology have been arranged under broad thematic headings. It will soon become clear, however, that many of them transcend such narrow groupings and could have readily been included in more than one section. It is not my intention to impose restrictions on these poems' possible meanings, so readers should feel free to discuss them under whatever heading seems appropriate. The form of a thematic anthology inevitably requires apparently arbitrary decisions to be taken about the placement of individual poems.

Within each broad, thematic section the poems are arranged into groups of two or three which contrast with or complement one another in some way. It is hoped that arranging poems in this way will provoke comment and make discussion easier. Some of the poems are very straightforward and accessible, others are much more demanding. The more challenging the poem, whether by way of unaccustomed style or complexity of meaning, the more comments and questions there are in the introduction to each section to help students make some headway with the poem.

The questions on each poem are not to be taken as part of a comprehension-type approach to poetry. They merely try to provide a 'way in', something to think about, to argue over or disagree with. In other words, they are stimuli for discussion and debate. They are intended to give students a purchase on each poem (especially the more challenging ones) and not to do their thinking for them. Once into a poem, students may go wherever they please. It is helpful, however, to consider factors like language, imagery, attitude, tone, diction, form, etc. and so the questions focus largely on these aspects.

The poems are deliberately drawn from all periods of English literature, including even the very earliest period, that of the Anglo-Saxons (AD 700–1000). They therefore offer clear illustrations of the different stylistic approaches that have prevailed in the writing of poetry in English during the last thousand years, though this was not the primary reason for their inclusion. Teachers may wish to highlight these different styles, awareness of which will help students when reading poetry in other, more conventional, anthologies.

Since the earliest recorded examples, English poetry has been written by women as well as by men, though few anthologies tend to reflect this fact. Even fewer reflect the wealth of material written by women over the centuries, material that has more than just curiosity value. Women poets have produced some very fine poems which deserve a wider audience than they have received so far. This anthology sets out to make such poetry more widely known, while reminding readers that the few poems included here represent, of necessity, only the tip of the iceberg of women's poetic achievement.

Clearly, some topics, such as being a parent, interest women poets more than their male counterparts. On the other hand, subjects usually thought to be of more interest to men, such as war and death, can and do take on an unexpected slant when they come under a woman's pen. Women, like men, have written on a variety of subjects and in a variety of styles and forms. Women, like men, have written poems that are amusing or moving. They have produced poems that enjoyed immense popularity in the past and poems that capture our imaginations today. As we shall see, women can write poems that are striking for their beauty or their elegance or their strangeness.

This is an anthology of poetry written by women in English, though it is not confined to English women poets. It includes poems by American (both black and white), Canadian and West Indian women. However, translations from cultures other than those that are English-speaking have not been included. This is partly because one of the defining characteristics of poetry is that it cannot be translated without loss. It is also because the book's focus lies in trying to trace English literary, cultural and ideological traditions as they impinged on women in the distant and more recent past. It may be that despite some common themes it is not possible, given the differences of class, race and lived historical moment, to trace an actual tradition of female authorship in the sense of one poet being influenced by, and building on, the work of a female predecessor, though this does begin to emerge in the nineteenth century. I have used the term 'tradition' more modestly, simply to convey the only recently acknowledged fact that women have been writing and publishing poetry for very much longer than most anthologies have led us to believe.

Finally, as there has been a vast amount of poetry to choose from, many fine poems have been omitted simply because space is limited. If readers' own favourites do not appear, it is not that they are not appreciated, but that the rigorous process of selection and omission has resulted in some inevitable omissions. It is hoped, however, that the present selection may surprise readers with new poems by women poets already known, as well as introduce readers to some women poets they have not encountered before. There are certainly some remarkable poems and poets contained within these pages.

Love and Passion

LOVE and passion are such common experiences that it would be very odd indeed if they did not figure prominently in poetry over the centuries. As in life, poetry about love encompasses an enormous range of emotion and experience. The women poets in this section approach the topic with as much variety as male poets have done. Some are surprisingly forthright and independent, considering that until changes in the law in the late nineteenth century, love could be much more of a poisoned chalice for women than for men because of their legally inferior status, particularly as wives. Marriage annulled at a stroke women's rights to their own money, property and even children, and conferred them on their husbands. This may not have been a problem with a husband who was loving and fair-minded, but would have become a tragedy of entrapment for a woman whose husband turned out to be profligate, promiscuous or cruel. Love has always been a lottery. What is surprising, perhaps, is that despite the many legal and social inequalities between men and women in the past, love and marriage still flourished.

Among women poets Elizabeth Barrett Browning is the supreme example of the unqualified triumph of mutual love and devotion which, as her first sonnet makes plain, snatched her from the jaws of death. At the advanced edge of 40 and after almost a lifetime of ill-health, she fell in love and eloped with a fellow poet against the wishes of her father, who had forbidden his children to marry and leave him. She paid a high price for her love as her father never communicated with her again, spurning all her attempts at reconciliation. But the Brownings' love proved steadfast in adversity. Elizabeth even died in her husband's arms 15 years later. She gave unabashed expression to the intense feeling Robert Browning inspired in her in a series of sonnets where she attempted to disguise the personal element by pretending they were translations 'from the Portuguese'. Although informed by joy, these sonnets have a wide emotional range. Sonnet XXXII is about her sense of her own unworthiness. For what does she praise her beloved in this sonnet? How does Sonnet XX differ? Is it self-critical, joyful, adoring? Look at the formal features of these sonnets. How do they break the mould of the male-dominated tradition of the sonnet form?

'On Monsieur's Departure' reveals Elizabeth I to have been as passionately in love as Elizabeth Barrett Browning, though this was no pleasurable experience for the queen. The poem presents her pre-dicament in a series of contradictory statements or paradoxes. Why is paradox such an appropriate device in this context? What picture of her emotional state does its use evoke?

Like Elizabeth I, who could not reveal her love, Eleanor Farjeon's Sonnet XLII suggests that her true feelings for Edward Thomas, the poet, were deeper than the simple friendship between them allowed. Her sense of unrequited love is expressed in Sonnet XXXIII. These two sonnets differ markedly in style and expression. Both are technically Shakespearean in that they end with a rhyming couplet, but the first is very modern and the second more clearly follows the master. Can you say what features set them apart?

'Cousin Kate', like 'A Man's Requirements' (page 44), involves the notorious double standard (and the betrayals it inevitably occasioned) by which it was perfectly permissible for men to have premarital or illicit sex but a disgrace for women to do the same. 'Cousin Kate' is the age-old story of a lowly bred girl being led astray by a titled landowner, but it has two unexpected twists in its plot. The poem suggests that there are other kinds of love that can exercise an important influence on life, not just the romantic and passionate. Try to pinpoint at least three kinds in the poem. Sylvia Townsend Warner's 'Fair, Do You Not See . . .' similarly extends our idea of love beyond romantic/passionate bounds. What kind of love does she depict in this poem?

Lady Mary Wortley Montagu reacts quite differently to passing sexual desires masquerading as love. 'An Answer to a Love-Letter', like 'The Lady's Yes', is about the rejection of male overtures, even a proposal of marriage. How do they differ? 'The Lady's Yes' is a cautionary tale. What is Elizabeth Barrett Browning advising and why? Given that in the mid-nineteenth century there was no divorce, so that marriage was for life, do you regard the lady as fickle, overly fastidious or far-sighted?

In total contrast, the next two poems are about love's intensity. Emily Brontë's 'Remembrance' is one of the most powerful and passionate expressions of romantic love in the language. How would you define romantic love on the basis of this poem? How does it compare with 'In June and Gentle Oven', the Canadian poet Anne Wilkinson's description of love's physical abandon on an Ontario farm? In what ways are the seasons used to parallel the feelings in these two poems?

Like Elizabeth Barrett Browning, Christina Rossetti also fell in love and was loved in return, but she felt obliged to reject marriage proposals from the two men she loved because of religious reservations. She also recorded her feelings in a series of sonnets. Compare her imagery and attitudes with those of Elizabeth Barrett Browning.

Three centuries earlier 'A Thousand Martyrs I Have Made' expressed the 'love them and leave them' approach to relations between the sexes. Is it possible to determine Aphra Behn's point of view in this poem? Is she claiming to be as promiscuous as men or is she giving voice, ironically, to what she sees as the emotionally exploitative male approach to women? Compare this poem with Edna St Vincent Millay's sonnet, which unequivocally expresses a modern, sexually liberated point of view. Which of the following words could you apply to each of these poems – cynical, satirical, joyless, happy, heartless?

This section ends with two poems that break with the stock motifs of the (male) courtly love tradition which have dominated the language of love poetry since the Middle Ages. In Sylvia Townsend Warner and Michael Field (the pseudonym of Katharine Bradley and Edith Cooper) there are no references to courtship, no love concealed, no hopeless longing, no roses, lilies or death, only the language of fluid and equal interchange (Townsend Warner) and of primal needs that antedate cultural practices (Field). Compare the vigour and natural-ness of these two poems with the earlier sonnets by Rossetti.

From SONNETS FROM THE PORTUGUESE

I

I thought once how Theocritus had sung
Of the sweet years, the dear and wished-for years,
Who each one in a gracious hand appears
To bear a gift for mortals, old or young:
And, as I mused it in his antique tongue,
I saw, in gradual vision through my tears,
The sweet, sad years, the melancholy years,
Those of my own life, who by turn had flung
A shadow across me. Straightway I was 'ware,
So weeping, how a mystic Shape did move
Behind me, and drew me backward by the hair;
And a voice said in mastery, while I strove, –
'Guess now who holds thee?' – 'Death', I said.
      But, there,
The silver answer rang, – 'Not Death, but Love.'

XX

Belovèd, my Belovèd, when I think
That thou wast in the world a year ago,
What time I sat alone here in the snow
And saw no footprint, heard the silence sink
No moment at thy voice, . . . but, link by link,
Went counting all my chains as if that so
They never could fall off at any blow
Struck by thy possible hand . . . why, thus I drink
Of life's great cup of wonder! Wonderful,
Never to feel thee thrill the day or night
With personal act or speech – nor even cull
Some prescience of thee with the blossoms white
Thou sawest growing! Atheists are as dull,
Who cannot guess God's presence out of sight.

XXXII

The first time that the sun rose on thine oath
To love me, I looked forward to the moon
To slacken all those bonds which seemed too soon
And quickly tied to make a lasting troth.
Quick-loving hearts, I thought, may quickly loathe;
And, looking on myself, I seemed not one
For such man's love! – more like an out-of-tune
Worn viol, a good singer would be wroth
To spoil his song with, and which, snatched in haste,
Is laid down at the first ill-sounding note.
I did not wrong myself so, but I placed
A wrong on *thee*. For perfect strains may float
'Neath master-hands, from instruments defaced –
And great souls, at one stroke, may do and dote.

ELIZABETH BARRETT BROWNING

ON MONSIEUR'S DEPARTURE

I grieve and dare not show my discontent,
I love and yet am forced to seem to hate,
I do, yet dare not say I ever meant,
I seem stark mute but inwardly do prate.
   I am and not, I freeze and yet am burned,
   Since from myself another self I turned.

My care is like my shadow in the sun,
Follows me flying, flies when I pursue it,
Stands and lies by me, doth what I have done.
His too familiar care doth make me rue it.
   No means I find to rid him from my breast,
   Till by the end of things it be supprest.

Some gentler passion slide into my mind,
For I am soft and made of melting snow;
Or be more cruel, love, and so be kind.
Let me or float or sink, be high or low.
   Or let me live with some more sweet content.
   Or die and so forget what love ere meant.

ELIZABETH I

SONNET XLII

When we had reached the bottom of the hill,
We said farewell, not as it were farewell,
But parting easily, as any will
To whom next day meeting is possible.
Why, it was on a scarcely-finished phrase
We made our clasp, and smiled, and turned away –
'I might meet you in London in three days.'
The backward look had soon no more to say.
You might. I thank you that you would not, friend.
Not thanks for sparing a pain I would have dared,
But for the change of mind which at the end
Acknowledged there was something to be spared,
    And parting not so light for you and me
    As you and I made it appear to be.

ELEANOR FARJEON

SONNET XXXIII

Love needs not two to render it complete,
O certainly love needs not even one!
Sweet singing wants no listener to be sweet,
And unseen light's still proper to the sun.
When sunlight falls upon unpeopled valleys
No presence can increase or dim its fall,
When nightingales sing in deserted alleys
No ear can make the night more musical.
    If solitary into the light and song
    I come, I know I have my treasure whole,
    Yea, and still have it whole, although a throng
    Runs after me down paths whereby I stole,
    Yea, and still have it whole, though only one
    Should follow me – or none, beloved, or none.

ELEANOR FARJEON

COUSIN KATE

I was a cottage-maiden
    Hardened by sun and air,
Contented with my cottage-mates,
    Not mindful I was fair.
Why did a great lord find me out
    And praise my flaxen hair?
Why did a great lord find me out
    To fill my heart with care?

He lured me to his palace-home –
    Woe's me for joy thereof –
To lead a shameless shameful life,
    His plaything and his love.
He wore me like a golden knot,
    He changed me like a glove:
So now I moan an unclean thing
    Who might have been a dove.

O Lady Kate, my Cousin Kate,
    You grow more fair than I:
He saw you at your father's gate,
    Chose you and cast me by.
He watched your steps along the lane,
    Your sport among the rye:
He lifted you from mean estate
    To sit with him on high.

Because you were so good and pure
    He bound you with his ring:
The neighbours call you good and pure,
    Call me an outcast thing.
Even so I sit and howl in dust
    You sit in gold and sing:
Now which of us has tenderer heart?
    You had the stronger wing.

O Cousin Kate, my love was true,
    Your love was writ in sand:
If he had fooled not me but you,
    If you stood where I stand,
He had not won me with his love
    Nor bought me with his land:
I would have spit into his face
    And not have taken his hand.

Yet I've a gift you have not got
    And seem not like to get:
For all your clothes and wedding-ring
    I've little doubt you fret.
My fair-haired son, my shame, my pride,
    Cling closer, closer yet:
Your sire would give broad lands for one
    To wear his coronet.

                    CHRISTINA ROSSETTI

'FAIR, DO YOU NOT SEE . . .'

'Fair, do you not see
How love has wasted me?'
'I am blind', said she.

'Blind only that youth
Knows not to look with ruth.'
'Blind, sir, in good sooth.

'Once it was not so.
My glance went to and fro,
Till I grew learned in woe.

'Blind-song larks I saw,
A rabbit in a snare's claw
That the rats did gnaw.

'Men, too I beheld
By iron engines quelled,
And a sapling felled.

'Then to the witch I sped.
Take out my eyes, I said,
Plant bright gems instead.'

SYLVIA TOWNSEND WARNER

AN ANSWER TO A LOVE-LETTER

Is it to me, this sad lamenting strain?
Are heaven's choicest gifts bestowed in vain?
A plenteous fortune, and a beauteous bride,
Your love rewarded, gratify'd your pride:
Yet leaving her – 'tis me that you pursue
Without one single charm, but being new.
How vile is man! how I detest their ways
Of artful falsehood, and designing praise!
Tasteless, an easy happiness you slight,
Ruin your joy, and mischief your delight,
Why should poor pug (the mimic of your kind)
Wear a rough chain, and be to box confin'd?
Some cup, perhaps, he breaks, or tears a fan
While roves unpunish'd the destroyer, man.
Not bound by vows, and unrestrain'd by shame,
In sport you break the heart, and rend the fame.
Not that your art can be successful here,
Th'already plunder'd need no robber fear:
Nor sighs, nor charms, nor flatteries can move,
Too well secur'd against a second love.
Once, and but once, that devil charm'd my mind;
To reason deaf, to observation blind;
I idly hoped (what cannot love persuade?)
My fondness equal'd, and my love repaid:
Slow to distrust, and willing to believe,
Long hush'd my doubts, and did myself deceive;
But oh! too soon – this tale would ever last;
Sleep, sleep my wrongs, and let me think them past.
For you, who mourn with counterfeited grief,
And ask so boldly like a begging thief,
May soon some other nymph inflict the pain,
You know so well with cruel art to feign.
Though long you sported with Dan Cupid's dart,
You may see eyes, and you may feel a heart.
So the brisk wits, who stop the evening coach,
Laugh at the fear which follows their approach;
With idle mirth, and haughty scorn despise
The passenger's pale cheek and staring eyes:
But seiz'd by Justice, find a fright no jest,
And all the terror doubled in their breast.

LADY MARY WORTLEY MONTAGU

THE LADY'S YES

I

'Yes,' I answered you last night;
  'No,' this morning, sir, I say.
Colours seen by candle-light
  Will not look the same by day.

II

When the viols played their best,
  Lamps above and laughs below,
Love me sounded like a jest,
  Fit for *yes* or fit for *no*.

III

Call me false or call me free –
  Vow, whatever light may shine,
No man on your face shall see
  Any grief for change on mine.

IV

Yet the sin is on us both;
  Time to dance is not to woo;
Wooing light makes fickle troth,
  Scorn of *me* recoils on *you*.

V

Learn to win a lady's faith
  Nobly as the thing is high,
Bravely, as for life and death –
  With a loyal gravity.

VI

Lead her from the festive boards,
  Point her to the starry skies;
Guard her, by your truthful words,
  Pure from courtship's flatteries.

VII

By your truth she shall be true,
  Ever true, as wives of yore;
And her *yes*, once said to you,
  Shall be Yes for evermore.

ELIZABETH BARRETT BROWNING

REMEMBRANCE

Cold in the earth and the deep snow piled above thee!
Far, far removed, cold in the dreary grave!
Have I forgot, my only Love, to love thee,
Severed at last by Time's all-wearing wave?

Now, when alone, do my thoughts no longer hover
Over the mountains, on Angora's shore,
Resting their wings where heath and fern-leaves cover
That noble heart for ever, ever more?

Cold in the earth, and fifteen wild Decembers,
From those brown hills have melted into spring –
Faithful, indeed, is the spirit that remembers
After such years of change and suffering!

Sweet Love of youth, forgive, if I forget thee
While the world's tide is bearing me along;
Sterner desires and darker hopes beset me,
Hopes which obscure but cannot do thee wrong!

No other sun has lightened up my heaven,
No other star has ever shone for me;
All my life's bliss from thy dear life was given,
All my life's bliss is in the grave with thee.

But, when the days of golden dreams had perished
And even Despair was powerless to destroy;
Then did I learn how existence could be cherished,
Strengthened and fed without the aid of joy;

Then did I check the tears of useless passion,
Weaned my young soul from yearning after thine;
Sternly denied its burning wish to hasten
Down to that tomb already more than mine.

And even yet, I dare not let it languish,
Dare not indulge in Memory's rapturous pain;
Once drinking deep of that divinest anguish,
How could I seek the empty world again?

EMILY BRONTË

'IN JUNE AND GENTLE OVEN'

In June and gentle oven
Summer kingdoms simmer
As they come

And flower and leaf and love
Release
Their sweetest juice.

No wind at all
On the wide green world
Where fields go strolling by
And in and out
An adder of a stream
Parts the daisies
On a small Ontario farm.

And where, in curve of meadow,
Lovers, touching, lie,
A church of grass stands up
And walls them, holy, in.

Fabulous the insects
Stud the air
Or walk on running water,
Klee-drawn saints
And bright as angels are.

Honeysuckle here
Is more than bees can bear
And time turns pale
And stops to catch its breath
And lovers slip their flesh
And light as pollen
Play on treble water
Till bodies reappear
And a shower of sun
To dry their languor.

Then two in one the lovers lie
And peel the skin of summer
With their teeth
And suck its marrow from a kiss
So charged with grace
The tongue, all knowing
Holds the sap of June
Aloof from seasons, flowing.

ANNE WILKINSON

MONNA INNOMINATA

SONNET II

I wish I could remember that first day,
   First hour, first moment of your meeting me,
   If bright or dim the season, it might be
Summer or Winter for aught I can say;
So unrecorded did it slip away,
   So blind was I to see and to foresee,
   So dull to mark the budding of my tree
That would not blossom yet for many a May.
If only I could recollect it, such
   A day of days! I let it come and go
   As traceless as a thaw of bygone snow;
It seemed to mean so little, meant so much;
If only now I could recall that touch,
   First touch of hand in hand – Did one but know!

SONNET VII

'Love me, for I love you' – and answer me,
   'Love me, for I love you': so shall we stand
   As happy equals in the flowering land
Of love, that knows not a dividing sea.
Love builds the house on rock and not on sand,
   Love laughs what while the winds rave desperately;
And who hath found love's citadel unmanned?
   And who hath held in bonds love's liberty? –
My heart's a coward though my words are brave –
   We meet so seldom, yet we surely part
   So often; there's a problem for your art!
   Still I find comfort in his Book who saith,
Though jealousy be cruel as the grave,
   And death be strong, yet love is strong as death.

SONNET XI

Many in aftertimes will say of you
   'He loved her' – while of me what will they say?
   Not that I loved you more than just in play,
For fashion's sake as idle women do.
Even let them prate; who know not what we knew
   Of love and parting in exceeding pain,
   Of parting hopeless here to meet again,
Hopeless on earth, and heaven is out of view.
But by my heart of love laid bare to you,
   My love that you can make not void nor vain,
Love that foregoes you but to claim anew
Beyond this passage of the gate of death,
   I charge you at the Judgment make it plain
My love of you was life and not a breath.

CHRISTINA ROSSETTI

SONG: A THOUSAND MARTYRS
I HAVE MADE

A thousand martyrs I have made,
　　All sacrific'd to my desire;
A thousand beauties have betray'd,
　　That languish in resistless fire.
The untam'd heart to hand I brought,
　　And fixed the wild and wandering thought.

I never vow'd nor sigh'd in vain
　　But both, tho' false, were well receiv'd.
The fair are pleas'd to give us pain,
　　And what they wish is soon believ'd.
And tho' I talk'd of wounds and smart,
　　Love's pleasures only touched my heart.

Alone the glory and the spoil
　　I always laughing bore away;
The triumphs, without pain or toil,
　　Without the hell, the heav'n of joy.
And while I thus at random rove
　　Despis'd the fools that whine for love.

APHRA BEHN

SONNET XLI

I, being born a woman and distressed
By all the needs and notions of my kind,
Am urged by your propinquity to find
Your person fair, and feel a certain zest
To bear your body's weight upon my breast:
So subtly is the fume of life designed,
To clarify the pulse and cloud the mind,
And leave me once again undone, possessed.
Think not for this, however, the poor treason
Of my stout blood against my staggering brain,
I shall remember you with love, or season
My scorn with pity, – let me make it plain:
I find this frenzy insufficient reason
For conversation when we meet again.

EDNA ST VINCENT MILLAY

I LOVE YOU WITH MY LIFE

I love you with my life – 'tis so I love you;
I give you as a ring
The cycle of my days till death:
I worship with the breath
That keeps me in the world with you and spring;
And God may dwell behind, but not above you.

Mine, in the dark, before the world's beginning:
The claim of every sense,
Secret and source of every need;
The goal to which I speed,
And at my heart a vigour more immense
Than will itself to urge me to its winning.

MICHAEL FIELD

DRAWING YOU, HEAVY WITH SLEEP

Drawing you, heavy with sleep to lie closer
Staying your poppy head upon my shoulder
It was as though I pulled the glide
Of a full river to my side.

Heavy with sleep and with sleep pliable,
You rolled at a touch towards me. Your arm fell
Across me as a river throws
An arm of flood across meadows.

And as the careless water its mirroring sanction
Grants to him at the river's brim long stationed,
Long drowned in thought, that yet he lives,
Since in that mirroring tide he moves,

Your body lying by mine to mine responded,
Your hair stirred on my mouth, my image was dandled
Deep in your sleep that flowed unstained
On from the image entertained.

SYLVIA TOWNSEND WARNER

Motherhood

THE following poems are about the experience of motherhood.
Each reflects a different aspect of what motherhood has
meant to women since the sixteenth century when, as Anne
Bradstreet's poem makes plain, giving birth was a very hazardous
experience for both mother and baby. Separated by three hundred
years, Anne Bradstreet (living in the new American colonies) and
Elaine Feinstein inevitably look at the forthcoming birth with different
preoccupations. Are there any similarities between their two poems?
Calliope was the Muse of epic poetry. Is she an appropriate figure to
evoke in such a context? How would you attempt to describe the tone
of these two poems – resigned, detached, apprehensive, fearful?

Fortunately for her family and herself Anne Bradstreet lived to be at
least sixty and to bear eight children. But death of babies at birth or
shortly after was in fact a common occurrence in Britain until quite
recently. Kathleen Raine, Alice Meynell and Katherine Philips all
explore maternal grief. Katherine Philips writes in the first person
about her own loss, while Alice Meynell allows the bereaved mother to
speak. Does this dramatic directness make their grief more vivid?
Does Kathleen Raine's more generalized, sibylline form of utterance
affect you equally, or less, profoundly?

Maternal grief is not, of course, confined to infant mortality.
Mothers of sons in particular have been vulnerable to the loss of their
older male children in time of war. The poems of Elizabeth Barrett
Browning, Alice Meynell and Frances Cornford illustrate this further
experience of bereavement. Frances Cornford's son, John, a poet and
scholar, was killed in action on his twenty-first birthday in 1936,
having volunteered to fight for the Republican cause in the Spanish
Civil War. Elizabeth Barrett Browning, who had suffered many
miscarriages and whose only child, a son, outlived her, imagines what
it would be like for a woman to lose two sons – her sole children –
fighting to defend a cause she supported. How would you describe the
very different tone of these two poems – angry, bitter, scornful,

helpless, reticent? How much do we learn about the kind of person each of these three young men was?

Alice Meynell's 'Parentage' is a less personal response to the deaths of sons in war than the two preceding poems. It is also unconventional in that grief has been displaced by guilt. Mothers are no longer helpless onlookers; they, like the fathers who take the fateful, political decisions, are implicated in the deaths. Where does Alice Meynell suggest the mothers' blame lies? It might help to consider the pun on the word 'bears'. Like her poem 'The Modern Mother' in the following group it is an unusual poem for its time (1896) in that it is less certain of the virtues of being a mother than the other poems here.

The two sonnets by Eleanor Farjeon and Elinor Wylie deal, like 'The Modern Mother', with less conspicuous aspects of motherhood. They examine the pain of never becoming a mother, or of having to act as a mother-substitute and nurse a parent incapacitated by grief or illness, or of being a less than devoted mother, guiltily aware of her own shortcomings. Why does Meynell's modern mother feel the need for 'forgiveness' rather than 'thanks?'

Finally, Anne Ridler and E. J. Scovell offer us something much more positive; the largely unalloyed joys of motherhood today, those pleasures and apprehensions even a father can share. Their poems seem to be as much a tribute to babyhood – the baby as an independent being – as about a mother's thoughts and feelings. 'Sick Boy' and 'Child Waking' illustrate this very well. Both are closely observed accounts of the baby or young child as a fully autonomous individual, yet both convey its vulnerability and its hovering mother's helplessness. How is this done? Look at the imagery of each poem. Why is Anne Ridler's imagery taken by and large from animal and plant life? What in the context is so unexpected about E. J. Scovell's imagery? Her talent has been described as 'domestic'. Is this a judgement you can agree with? In 'The First Year' what values does she see in becoming a mother? How does she take her poems beyond the domestic/maternal scene which gives rise to them? Are there any phrases or sentences in 'The First Year' that strike you as particularly apt or interesting?

BEFORE THE BIRTH OF ONE OF HER CHILDREN

All things within this fading world hath end,
Adversity doth still our joys attend;
No ties so strong, no friends so dear and sweet,
But with death's parting blow is sure to meet.
The sentence past is most irrevocable,
A common thing, yet oh, inevitable.
How soon, my Dear, death may my steps attend,
How soon't may be thy lot to lose thy friend,
We both are ignorant, yet love bids me
These farewell lines to recommend to thee,
That when that knot's untied that made us one,
I may seem thine, who in effect am none.
And if I see not half my days that's due,
What nature would, God grant to yours and you;
The many faults that well you know I have
Let be interred in my oblivious grave;
If any worth or virtue were in me,
Let that live freshly in thy memory
And when thou feel'st no grief, as I no harms,
Yet love thy dead, who long lay in thine arms.
And when thy loss shall be repaid with gains
Look to my little babes, my dear remains.
And if thou love thyself, or loved'st me,
These O protect from step-dame's injury.
And if chance to thine eyes shall bring this verse,
With some sad sighs honour my absent hearse;
And kiss this paper for thy love's dear sake,
Who with salt tears this last farewell did take.

ANNE BRADSTREET

CALLIOPE IN THE LABOUR WARD

she who has no love for women
married and housekeeping

now the bird notes begin
in the blood in the June morning
look how these ladies are
as little squeamish as
men in a great war

have come into their bodies
as their brain dwindles to
the silver circle on
eyelids under sun
and time opens
pain in the shallows to wave up and over them

grunting in gas and air
they sail to a
darkness without self
where no will reaches

in that abandon less
than human
give birth
bleak as a goddess

ELAINE FEINSTEIN

MATERNAL GRIEF

I am not human,
I am not human,
Nor am I divine.

To whom,
to whom can I cry,
'I am thine'?

I have picked my grandsire's corpse to the bone
I have found no ghost in brisket or chine.
I have shed the blood of my female kin,
but they never return to speak again.

I am not human,
I am not human,
How shall I feed my hungry children?

I make the porridge of meal and wine
and pour it out in the troughs for swine.

The ghosts are hungry, the ghosts are divine,
but the pigs eat the meal, and the priests drink the wine.

KATHLEEN RAINE

MATERNITY

One wept whose only child was dead,
  New-born, ten years ago.
'Weep not; he is in bliss,' they said.
  She answered, 'Even so,

'Ten years ago was born in pain
  A child, not now forlorn.
But oh, ten years ago, in vain,
  A mother, a mother was born.'

ALICE MEYNELL

ORINDA UPON LITTLE HECTOR PHILIPS

Twice forty months of wedlock I did stay,
Then had my vows crown'd with a lovely boy,
And yet in forty days he dropt away,
O swift vicissitude of human joy.

I did but see him and he disappear'd,
I did but pluck the rose-bud and it fell,
A sorrow unforeseen and scarcely fear'd,
For ill can mortals their afflictions spell.

And now (sweet babe) what can my trembling heart
Suggest to right my doleful fate or thee,
Tears are my Muse and sorrow all my art,
So piercing groans must be thy elegy.

Thus whilst no eye is witness of my moan,
I grieve thy loss (Ah boy too dear to live)
And let the unconcerned world alone,
Who neither will, nor can refreshment give.

An off'ring too for thy sad tomb I have,
Too just a tribute to thy early hearse,
Receive these gasping numbers to thy grave,
The last of thy unhappy mother's verse.

KATHERINE PHILIPS

MOTHER AND POET

(TURIN, AFTER NEWS FROM GAETA, 1861)

I

Dead! One of them shot by the sea in the east,
   And one of them shot in the west by the sea.
Dead! both my boys! When you sit at the feast
   And are wanting a great song for Italy free,
      Let none look at *me*!

II

Yet I was a poetess only last year,
   And good at my art, for a woman, men said;
But *this* woman, *this*, who is agonised here,
   – The east sea and west sea rhyme on in her head
      For ever instead.

III

What art can a woman be good at? Oh, vain!
   What art *is* she good at, but hurting her breast
With the milk-teeth of babes, and a smile at the pain?
   Ah boys, how you hurt! you were strong as you pressed,
      And I proud, by that test.

IV

What art's for a woman? To hold on her knees
   Both darlings! to feel all their arms round her throat,
Cling, strangle a little! to sew by degrees
   And 'broider the long-clothes and neat little coat;
      To dream and to doat.

V

To teach them . . . It stings there! *I* made them indeed
   Speak plain the word *country*. *I* taught them, no doubt,
That a country's a thing men should die for at need.
   I prated of liberty, rights, and about
      The tyrant cast out.

VI

And when their eyes flashed . . . O my beautiful eyes! . . .
   I exulted; nay, let them go forth at the wheels
Of the guns, and denied not. But then the surprise
   When one sits quite alone! Then one weeps, then one kneels!
      God, how the house feels!

VII

At first, happy news came, in gay letters moiled
   With my kisses, – of camp-life and glory, and how
They both loved me; and, soon coming home to be spoiled
   In return would fan off every fly from my brow
      With their green laurel-bough.

VIII

Then was triumph at Turin: 'Ancona was free!'
   And some one came out of the cheers in the street,
With a face pale as stone, to say something to me.
   My Guido was dead! I fell down at his feet,
      While they cheered in the street.

IX

I bore it; friends soothed me; my grief looked sublime
   As the ransom of Italy. One boy remained
To be leant on and walked with, recalling the time
   When the first grew immortal, while both of us strained
      To the height he had gained.

X

And letters still came, shorter, sadder, more strong,
   Writ now but in one hand, 'I was not to faint, –
One loved me for two – would be with me ere long:
   And *Viva l'Italia!* – *he* died for, our saint,
      Who forbids our complaint.'

XI

My Nanni would add, 'he was safe, and aware
   Of a presence that turned off the balls, – was imprest
It was Guido himself, who knew what I could bear,
   And how 'twas impossible, quite dispossessed
      To live on for the rest.'

XII

On which, without pause, up the telegraph line
   Swept smoothly the next news from Gaeta: – *Shot.*
Tell his mother. Ah, ah, 'his', 'their' mother, – not 'mine',
   No voice says '*My* mother' again to me. What!
      You think Guido forgot?

XIII

Are souls straight so happy that, dizzy with Heaven,
   They drop earth's affections, conceive not of woe?
I think not. Themselves were too lately forgiven
   Through THAT Love and Sorrow which reconciled so
      The Above and Below.

XIV

O Christ of the five wounds, who look'dst through the dark
   To the face of Thy mother! consider, I pray,
How we common mothers stand desolate, mark,
   Whose sons, not being Christs, die with eyes turned away,
      And no last word to say!

XV

Both boys dead? but that's out of nature. We all
   Have been patriots, yet each house must always keep one.
'Twere imbecile, hewing out roads to a wall;
   And, when Italy's made, for what end is it done
      If we have not a son?

XVI

Ah, ah, ah! when Gaeta's taken, what then?
   When the fair wicked queen sits no more at her sport
Of the fire-balls of death crashing souls out of men?
   When the guns of Cavalli with final retort
      Have cut the game short?

XVII

When Venice and Rome keep their new jubilee,
   When your flag takes all heaven for its white, green, and red,
When *you* have your country from mountain to sea,
   When King Victor has Italy's crown on his head,
      (And *I* have my Dead) –

XVIII

What then? Do not mock me. Ah, ring your bells low,
  And burn your lights faintly! *My* country is *there*,
Above the star pricked by the last peak of snow:
  My Italy's THERE, with my brave civic Pair,
    To disfranchise despair!

XIX

Forgive me. Some women bear children in strength,
  And bite back the cry of their pain in self-scorn;
But the birth-pangs of nations will wring us at length
  Into wail such as this – and we sit on forlorn
    When the man-child is born.

XX

Dead! One of them shot by the sea in the east,
  And one of them shot in the west by the sea.
Both! both my boys! If in keeping the feast
  You want a great song for your Italy free,
    Let none look at *me*!

ELIZABETH BARRETT BROWNING

PARENTAGE

*'When Augustus Cæsar legislated against the unmarried citizens of Rome,
he declared them to be, in some sort, slayers of the people.'*

  Ah! no, not these!
These, who were childless, are not they who gave
So many dead unto the journeying wave,
The helpless nurslings of the cradling seas;
Not they who doomed by infallible decrees
Unnumbered man to the innumerable grave.

  But those who slay
Are fathers. Theirs are armies. Death is theirs –
The death of innocences and despairs;
The dying of the golden and the grey.
The sentence, when these speak it, has no Nay.
And she who slays is she who bears, who bears.

ALICE MEYNELL

THE SCHOLAR

You often went to breathe a timeless air
And walk with those you loved, perhaps the most.
You spoke to Plato. You were native there.
Like one who made blind Homer sing to him,
You visited the caves where sirens swim
Their deep indented coast.
                      With us you seemed
A quiet happy sailor come of late
From those strange seas you best could navigate,
Knowing a world that others only dreamed.
Almost we looked for spray upon your hair,
Who met you, silent-footed on the stair,
Like an Elysian ghost.
                    So on that day
You left us on a deep withdrawing tide,
We dared not beg you, with one sigh, to stay
Or turn from your discoveries aside.

FRANCES CORNFORD

SONNET XXVIII

Farewell, you children that I might have borne.
Now must I put you from me year by year,
Now year by year the root of life be torn
Out of the womb to which you were so dear,
Now year by year the milky springs be dried
Within the sealed-up fountains of my breast,
Now year by year be to my arms denied
The burden they would ache with and be blessed.
Sometimes I felt your lips and hands so close
I almost could have plucked you from the dark,
But now your very dream more distant grows
As my still aching body grows more stark.
I shall not see you laugh or hear you weep,
Kiss you awake, or cover up your sleep.

ELEANOR FARJEON

SONNET XII

In our content, before the autumn came
To shower sallow droppings on the mould,
Sometimes you have permitted me to fold
Your grief in swaddling-bands, and smile to name
Yourself my infant, with an infant's claim
To utmost adoration as of old,
Suckled with kindness, fondled from the cold,
And loved beyond philosophy or shame.

I dreamt I was the mother of a son
Who had deserved a manger for a crib;
Torn from your body, furbished from your rib;
I am the daughter of your skeleton,
Born of your bitter and excessive pain:
I shall not dream you are my child again.

ELINOR WYLIE

THE MODERN MOTHER

Oh, what a kiss
With filial passion overcharged is this!
To this misgiving breast
This child runs, as a child ne'er ran to rest
Upon the light heart and the unoppressed.

Unhoped, unsought!
A little tenderness, this mother thought
The utmost of her meed.
She looked for gratitude; content indeed
With thus much that her nine years' love had bought.

Nay, even with less.
This mother, giver of life, death, peace, distress,
Desired ah! not so much
Thanks as forgiveness; and the passing touch
Expected, and the slight, the brief caress.

O filial light
Strong in these childish eyes, these new, these bright
Intelligible stars! Their rays
Are near the constant earth, guides in the maze,
Natural, true, keen in this dusk of days.

ALICE MEYNELL

SICK BOY

Illness falls like a cloud upon
　My little frisking son:
He lies like a plant under a blight
　Dulling the bright leaf-skin.
Our culture falls away, the play
　That apes, and grows, a man,
Falters, and like the wounded or
　Sick animal, his kin,
He curls to shelter the flame of life
　And lies close in his den.

Children in patient suffering
　Are sadder to see than men
Because more humble and more bewildered:
　What words can there explain
Why all pleasures have lost their savour,
　Or promise health again?
Kindness speaks from a far mountain –
　Cannot touch their pain.

ANNE RIDLER

CHILD WAKING

The child sleeps in the daytime,
With his abandoned, with his jetsam look,
On the bare mattress, across the cot's corner;
Covers and toys thrown out, a routine labour.

Relaxed in sleep and light,
Face upwards, never so clear a prey to eyes;
Like a walled town surprised out of the air –
All life called in, yet all laid bare

To the enemy above –
He has taken cover in daylight, gone to ground
In his own short length, his body strong in bleached
Blue cotton and his arms outstretched.

Now he opens eyes but not
To see at first; they reflect the light like snow,
And I wait in doubt if he sleeps or wakes, till I see
Slight pain of effort at the boundary

And hear how the trifling wound
Of bewilderment fetches a caverned cry
As he crosses out of sleep – at once to recover
His place and poise, and smile as I lift him over.

But I recall the blue-
White snowfield of his eyes empty of sight
High between dream and day, and think how there
The soul might rise visible as a flower.

E. J. SCOVELL

THE FIRST YEAR

II

Before she first had smiled or looked with calm
Light-answering eyes and claimed to be of man
I put my finger in her shadowy palm,
And her own whispering ones from their chestnut fan
Closed again (as they must) on mine, to a bud.
Then I was where strong currents piled and slackened.
Like a pulse telling all the power of blood
This palm seemed the cavern where alone her darkened
And secret rock-roofed river showed to man
(Except when one inside half-raised the blind
Of her inky eyes, and fierce a dark beam ran
Searchlighting day). So I strayed on her mind;
And thought I trespassed in that covered land.
Her hand seemed private, still an unborn hand.

VI

I am absorbed and clouded by a sensual love
Of one whose soul is sense and flesh the substance of
Her spirit; and her thoughts, like grass shadowed by the wind's flight,
Her hands' bemused and under-water dance in light.

· ·

When I serve her (whose sense is soul) I serve her all,
Whose feeding is her love, whose mind in bone grows tall;
  And watching her (whose thoughts move without words like wind on
    grass)
I am less than I was my own; I am not what I was.

XI

When the old sleep, a sadness moves beholders;
And when the strong mature, whose shoulders
Support the world in their generation's hour –
Strangely sleep's weakness lies with power;
But when you sleep, sleep only seems your other
Self, your flower's leaf, your brother.

Sleep's unknowing, where so little's known,
Is a lamb with a lamb lying down.
And sleep's imprudence and unguarded nature
You wear like any thornless creature,
Open, upturned to dangerous nights and days
Like scabious where the cattle graze.

Not fast like ours your categories seem;
Your dreams play with your waking dream.
And bold all visions come into your net –
The rage of thought not on you yet,
That frightens the many to a standing stone
So it may seize and have the one.

Not at the pillow end of your big bed
You sleep, but where your wandering head
Happens to tire and rest. So sometimes, thrown
Far out on your blue eiderdown,
You seem a sleeping sea-bird, guarded best
By yielding to the sea, wild sea its friend and nest.

E. J. SCOVELL

Relations Between the Sexes

LOVE and passion are not the only emotions to surface in relations between the sexes. Mutual incompatibility as well as the many social and legal inequalities between men and women in the past have occasioned frustration, anger, distress and a host of other negative emotions.

Until women were allowed access to the same educational facilities and opportunities as men and permitted to enjoy the same legal and political rights, their relationships with men and their sense of their own worth were likely to be affected one way or another. The more spirited and literate women were not easily convinced of their 'natural' inferiority even if it was enshrined in statute. Female inequality in marriage led women writers in particular to liken marriage to a state of slavery. For example, on marriage a middle-class woman's whole estate – everything she possessed – passed into her husband's keeping for good, to do with as he thought fit. Even her children were deemed to belong to him, so that if she left him on justifiable grounds of cruelty or promiscuity she was entitled neither to take the children with her nor to see them again. It was only in the latter part of the nineteenth century, with the passage of legislation like the Married Women's Property Acts (1870 and 1882), that women's rights in the fundamental matter of their personal independence began to be addressed. The issue of female suffrage, though long fought for, did not become a reality until 1918 when women had proved they could adequately fill the places of their absent (and dead) sons, brothers and husbands in the country's economy.

The first female complaint in the language is found more than a thousand years ago in the Anglo-Saxon period. 'The Wife's Lament' strikes a note that even we in the late twentieth century can appreciate. Her situation is not historically determined, though it is somewhat puzzling because it is largely unexplained. What is clear is that interfering relatives have driven a wedge between husband and wife. The poem is an elegy, which strictly speaking is a lament for the loss of someone dear through death. Here, the wife laments her enforced separation from her husband, who has been misled by his relatives into banishing her. She recalls her previous happiness and regrets the loss of her lord. Note the very special style in which this poem is written. There was no rhyme in Anglo-Saxon poetry, its distinguishing feature being frequent alliteration. Compare 'The Wife's Lament' with Anna Wickham's 'The Homecoming', which is also about emotional, though not physical, separation within a marriage. Which of the two do you find the more moving and why? What effect do the insistent rhythm and rhyme have in 'The Homecoming'? Do you think they detract from the tragedy or reinforce it?

In the early eighteenth century Lady Mary Chudleigh pictured marriage as a state akin to servitude in 'To the Ladies' and recommended women avoid it. 'The Man With a Hammer' offers an additional gloss on the disadvantages of marriage which is taken up and expanded in 'The Emulation'. What do these two poems find so objectionable about the married state? How does the imagery of 'The Man with a Hammer' convey its critical viewpoint? Do you think the poem's even and unemotional tone makes it more or less effective?

Becoming a blue-stocking, or a learned, literary woman, had its problems too, as Mary Elizabeth Coleridge (a great-niece of Samuel Taylor Coleridge) suggests in 'A Clever Woman'. She has taken up the intellectual and literary pursuits 'The Emulation' recommends, but her plight is still piteous. What is the problem here for the woman and for the man she loves? Notice how 'A Clever Woman' is written in the first person. This can be a powerful way of writing because it is very direct and immediate. 'The 'Witch' is also written in the first person but presents a less individualized picture. Do you find it any the less effective or striking? Do you know the historical events at Salem, Massachusetts, that it refers to?

Both 'The Farmer's Bride' and 'A Man's Requirements' allow the male voice to be heard in relations between the sexes. By the end of 'The Farmer's Bride' do you feel sorry for the farmer? How does his attitude change from the first three lines to the last three lines of the poem? Although the poem is told in the first person and from the farmer's point of view, we still feel most sympathy for his bride. How is this achieved by the poet? In 'A Man's Requirements' Elizabeth Barrett Browning adopts the male voice to expose the notorious double standard in relations between men and women. How can we tell her tone is ironic?

Christina Rossetti's 'Maude Clare' features just such a duplicitous male as Elizabeth Barrett Browning lampoons. The simple ballad form and the traditional ballad story of betrayed love undermine the romantic devotion that convention suggests women want. What does marriage mean for Nell? What does love mean for the speaker in Emily Dickinson's 'The Contract'? Does she explode romantic illusions by using the language of a commercial transaction, reflecting what marriage so often was in the real world? If so, how can the poem retain its erotic charge?

Not all relations between the sexes have been marred by unhappiness or duplicity. George Eliot wrote a series of eleven Shakespearean sonnets called *Brother and Sister* about her childhood relationship with her brother, Isaac. Sadly, in adulthood he became estranged from her because of her unorthodox relationship with G. H. Lewes. These sonnets (three of which are included here, with a fourth appearing in the section 'Separation and Suffering') pay tribute to the immense personal enrichment George Eliot felt she and her brother had derived from their childhood devotion to each other. In what ways does she suggest it enriched their lives both then and later? How lasting does she feel the effects of their love were? What humorous/ironic touch in sonnet 1 enables us to share her sense of childish dependence?

'Woman's Song' is written in the form of a prayer in which the poet asks the trappings of a typical housewife's life to intercede for her. What does she want them to do? At first sight the poem looks like a feminist protest about woman's domestic lot, but it does not in fact suggest these trappings are a burden. Although the poem's theme is a serious one, would you agree that it is expressed in a witty, humorous way?

Finally, E. J. Scovell and Anne Stevenson write in celebration of marriage. E. J. Scovell's sonnet 'Marriage and Death' pays tribute to her own marriage and the intermingling of selves or souls that it involves. What unusual advantage does she seem to suggest it might confer? An epithalamium is a poem in honour of a particular marriage. In celebrating the wedding of her friends, Anne Stevenson plays with some key words and ideas. What are they and how does she highlight them? Do they change their meaning through the poem? The mention of the housewifely job of 'cleaning' links the poem with 'Woman's Song'. Can you find any other points of comparison between these two poems?

THE WIFE'S LAMENT

I sing of myself, a sorrowful woman,
of my own unhap. All I have felt,
since I grew up, of ill let me say,
be it new or old – never more than now:
I have borne the cross of my cares, always.

First my friend went far from home,
over the waves; I was awake at dawn,
I wondered where he was, day and night.
Then I went out, unhappy wife,
lonely and wretched, looking for fellowship.

The man's kindred, with minds of darkness,
began to plot to part us two,
that we might lead a life most hateful,
live most aloof, and I longed for him.

My lord bade me lodge in this hut.
Little I know of love-making here,
of sweet friendship. My soul is mournful
to find my man, my friend, my mate
heavy-hearted, happy not at all,
hiding his mood, harbouring ill
under a blithe bearing. We both made vow
that death alone should drive us asunder
naught else in the world; that was, but is no more;
it is now as if it had never been,
that friendship of ours. Far and nigh now
I must bear the hate of my best beloved.

They drove me out to dwell in the woods
under an oak tree, in that old stone-heap.
Fallen is this house; I am filled with yearning.

The dales are dim, the downs are high,
the bitter yards with briars are grown,
the seats are sorrowful. I am sick at heart,
he is so far from me. There are friends on earth,
lovers living that lie together,
while I, early and all alone,
walk under the oak tree, wander through these halls.
There I must sit the summerlong day,
there I can rue my wretchedness,
bewail my many woes, my hardships
for I cannot rest from my cares ever,
nor from all the longing that in this life befell me.

It is the way of a young man to be woeful in mood,
hard in his heart's thought; to have, besides,
a blithe bearing and a breast full of care,
a throng of woes alike when his worldly bliss
belongs all to him and when he lives an outcast
in a far country. My friend is sitting,
a cliff for shelter, cold in the storm,
a friend weary in mood, flooded with water
in his dismal dwelling, doomed to sorrow.

That man, my friend, is mindful too often
of a happier house. Hard is the lot
of one that longs for love in vain.

Translated by KEMP MALONE

THE HOMECOMING

I waited ten years in the husk
That once had been our home,
Watching from dawn to dusk
To see if he would come.

And there he was beside me
Always at board and bed;
I looked – and woe betide me
He I had loved was dead.

He fell at night on the hillside,
They brought him home to his place,
I had not the solace of sorrow
Till I had looked at his face.

Then I clasped the broken body
To see it if breathed or moved,
For there, in the smile of his dying,
Was the gallant man I had loved.

O wives come lend me your weeping,
I have not enough of tears,
For he is dead who was sleeping
These ten accursed years.

ANNA WICKHAM

TO THE LADIES

Wife and servant are the same,
But only differ in the name:
For when that fatal knot is tied,
Which nothing, nothing can divide,
When she the word *Obey* has said,
And man by law supreme has made,
Then all that's kind is laid aside,
And nothing left but state and pride.
Fierce as an eastern prince he grows,
And all his innate rigour shows:
Then but to look, to laugh, or speak,
Will the nuptial contract break.
Like mutes, she signs alone must make,
And never any freedom take,
But still be governed by a nod,
And fear her husband as her god:
Him still must serve, him still obey,
And nothing act, and nothing say,
But what her haughty lord thinks fit,
Who, with the power, has all the wit.
Then shun, oh! shun that wretched state,
And all the fawning flatt'rers hate.
Value yourselves, and men despise:
You must be proud, if you'll be wise.

LADY MARY CHUDLEIGH

THE MAN WITH A HAMMER

My Dear was a mason
And I was his stone.
And quick did he fashion
A house of his own.

As fish in the waters,
As birds in a tree,
So natural and blithe lives
His spirit in me.

ANNA WICKHAM

THE EMULATION

Say, tyrant Custom, why must we obey
The impositions of thy haughty sway?
From the first dawn of life unto the grave,
Poor womankind's in every state a slave,
The nurse, the mistress, parent and the swain,
For love she must, there's none escape that pain.
Then comes the last, the fatal slavery:
The husband with insulting tyranny
Can have ill manners justified by law,
For men all join to keep the wife in awe.
Moses, who first our freedom did rebuke,
Was married when he writ the Pentateuch.
They're wise to keep us slaves, for well they know,
If we were loose, we soon should make them so.
We yield like vanquished kings whom fetters bind,
When chance of war is to usurpers kind;
Submit in form; but they'd our thoughts control,
And lay restraints on the impassive soul.
They fear we should excel their sluggish parts,
Should we attempt the sciences and arts;
Pretend they were designed for them alone,
So keep us fools to raise their own renown.
Thus priests of old, their grandeur to maintain,
Cried vulgar eyes would sacred laws profane;
So kept the mysteries behind a screen:
Their homage and the name were lost had they been seen.
But in this blessèd age such freedom's given,
That every man explains the will of heaven;
And shall we women now sit tamely by,
Make no excursions in philosophy,
Or grace our thoughts in tuneful poetry?
We will our rights in learning's world maintain;
Wit's empire now shall know a female reign.
Come, all ye fair, the great attempt improve,
Divinely imitate the realms above:
There's ten celestial females govern wit,
And but two gods that dare pretend to it.
And shall these finite males reverse their rules?
No, we'll be wits, and then men must be fools.

SARAH FYGE EGERTON

A CLEVER WOMAN

You thought I had the strength of men,
　Because with men I dared to speak,
And courted science now and then,
　And studied Latin for a week;
But woman's woman, even when
　She reads her Ethics in the Greek.

You thought me wiser than my kind;
　You thought me 'more than common tall';
You thought because I had a mind,
　That I could have no heart at all;
But woman's woman you will find,
　Whether she be great or small.

And then you needs must die – ah, well!
　I knew you not, you loved not me.
'Twas not because that darkness fell,
　You saw not what there was to see.
But I that saw and could not tell –
　O evil Angel, set me free!

MARY ELIZABETH COLERIDGE

THE WITCH

When I was a girl by Nilus stream
　I watched the desert stars arise;
My lover, he who dreamed the Sphinx,
　Learned all his dreaming from my eyes.

I bore in Greece a burning name,
　And I have been in Italy
Madonna to a painter-lad,
　And mistress to a Medici.

And have you heard (and I have heard)
　Of puzzled men with decorous mien,
Who judged – The wench knows far too much –
　And hanged her on the Salem green?

ADELAIDE CRAPSEY

THE FARMER'S BRIDE

Three Summers since I chose a maid,
Too young maybe – but more's to do
At harvest-time than bide and woo.
  When us was wed she turned afraid
Of love and me and all things human;
Like the shut of a winter's day.
Her smile went out, and 'twasn't a woman –
  More like a little frightened fay.
    One night, in the Fall, she runned away.

'Out 'mong the sheep, her be,' they said,
Should properly have been abed;
But sure enough she wasn't there
Lying awake with her wide brown stare.
So over seven-acre field and up-along across the down
We chased her, flying like a hare
Before our lanterns. To Church-Town
    All in a shiver and a scare
We caught her, fetched her home at last
    And turned the key upon her, fast.

She does the work about the house
As well as most, but like a mouse:
    Happy enough to chat and play
    With birds and rabbits and such as they,
    So long as men-folk keep away.
'Not near, not near!' her eyes beseech
When one of us comes within reach.
    The women say that beasts in stall
    Look round like children at her call.
    I've hardly heard her speak at all,
Shy as a leveret, swift as he,
Straight and slight as a young larch tree,
Sweet as the first wild violets, she,
To her wild self. But what to me?

The short days shorten and the oaks are brown:
   The blue smoke rises to the low grey sky,
One leaf in the still air falls slowly down,
   A magpie's spotted feathers lie
On the black earth spread white with rime,
The berries redden up to Christmas-time.
   What's Christmas-time without there be
   Some other in the house than we!

She sleeps up in the attic there
   Alone, poor maid. 'Tis but a stair
Betwixt us. Oh! my God! the down,
The soft young down of her, the brown,
The brown of her – her eyes, her hair, her hair!

CHARLOTTE MEW

A MAN'S REQUIREMENTS

I

Love me, Sweet, with all thou art,
   Feeling, thinking, seeing;
Love me in the lightest part,
   Love me in full being.

II

Love me with thine open youth
   In its frank surrender;
With the vowing of thy mouth.
   With its silence tender.

III

Love me with thine azure eyes,
   Made for earnest granting;
Taking colour from the skies,
   Can Heaven's truth be wanting?

IV

Love me with their lids, that fall
   Snow-like at first meeting;
Love me with thine heart, that all
   Neighbours then see beating.

V

Love me with thine hand stretched out
    Freely – open-minded;
Love me with thy loitering foot, –
    Hearing one behind it.

VI

Love me with thy voice, that turns
    Sudden faint above me;
Love me with thy blush that burns
    When I murmur *Love me!*

VII

Love me with thy thinking soul,
    Break it to love-sighing;
Love me with thy thoughts that roll
    On through living – dying.

VIII

Love me in thy gorgeous airs,
    When the world has crowned thee;
Love me, kneeling at thy prayers,
    With the angels round thee.

IX

Love me pure, as musers do,
    Up the woodlands shady:
Love me gaily, fast and true,
    As a winsome lady.

X

Through all hopes that keep us brave,
    Farther off or nigher,
Love me for the house and grave,
    And for something higher.

XI

Thus, if thou wilt prove me, Dear,
    Woman's love no fable,
I will love *thee* – half a year –
    As a man is able.

ELIZABETH BARRETT BROWNING

MAUDE CLARE

Out of the church she followed them
  With a lofty step and mien:
His bride was like a village maid,
  Maude Clare was like a queen.

'Son Thomas,' his lady mother said,
  With smiles, almost with tears:
'May Nell and you but live as true
  As we have done for years;

'Your father thirty years ago
  Had just your tale to tell;
But he was not so pale as you,
  Nor I so pale as Nell.'

My lord was pale with inward strife,
  And Nell was pale with pride;
My lord gazed long on pale Maude Clare
  Or ever he kissed the bride.

'Lo, I have brought my gift, my lord,
  Have brought my gift,' she said:
'To bless the hearth, to bless the board,
  To bless the marriage-bed.

'Here's my half of the golden chain
  You wore about your neck,
That day we waded ankle-deep
  For lilies in the beck:

'Here's my half of the faded leaves
  We plucked from budding bough,
With feet amongst the lily leaves, –
  The lilies are budding now.'

He strove to match her scorn with scorn,
  He faltered in his place:
'Lady,' he said, – 'Maude Clare,' he said, –
  'Maude Clare:' – and hid his face.

She turn'd to Nell: 'My Lady Nell,
   I have a gift for you;
Though, were it fruit, the bloom were gone.
   Or, were it flowers, the dew.

'Take my share of a fickle heart,
   Mine of a paltry love:
Take it or leave it as you will,
   I wash my hands thereof.'

'And what you leave,' said Nell, 'I'll take,
   And what you spurn, I'll wear;
For he's my lord for better and worse,
   And him I love, Maude Clare.

'Yea, though you're taller by the head,
   More wise, and much more fair;
I'll love him till he loves me best,
   Me best of all, Maude Clare.'

               CHRISTINA ROSSETTI

THE CONTRACT

I gave myself to him,
   And took himself for pay.
The solemn contract of a life
   Was ratified this way.

The wealth might disappoint,
   Myself a poorer prove
Than this great purchaser suspect,
   The daily own of Love

Depreciate this vision;
   But, till the merchant buy,
Still fable, in the isles of spice,
   The subtle cargoes lie.

At least, 'tis mutual risk, –
   Some found it mutual gain;
Sweet debt of Life, – each night to owe,
   Insolvent, every noon.

               EMILY DICKINSON

From BROTHER AND SISTER SONNETS

I

I cannot choose but think upon the time
When our two lives grew like two buds that kiss
At lightest thrill from the bee's swinging chime,
Because the one so near the other is.

He was the elder and a little man
Of forty inches, bound to show no dread,
And I the girl that puppy-like now ran,
Now lagged behind my brother's larger tread.

I held him wise, and when he talked to me
Of snakes and birds, and which God loved the best,
I thought his knowledge marked the boundary
Where men grew blind, though angels knew the rest.

If he said 'Hush!' I tried to hold my breath
Wherever he said 'Come!' I stepped in faith.

5

Thus rambling we were schooled in deepest lore,
And learned the meanings that give words a soul,
The fear, the love, the primal passionate store,
Whose shaping impulses make manhood whole.

Those hours were seed to all my after good;
My infant gladness, through eye, ear and touch,
Took easily as warmth a various food
To nourish the sweet skill of loving much.

For who in age shall roam the earth and find
Reason for loving that will strike out love
With sudden rod from the hard year-pressed mind?
Were reasons sown as thick as stars above,

'Tis love must see them, as the eye sees light:
Day is but Number to the darkened sight.

9

We had the self-same world enlarged for each
By loving difference of girl and boy:
The fruit that hung on high beyond my reach
He plucked for me, and oft he must employ

A measuring glance to guide my tiny shoe
Where lay firm stepping-stones, or call to mind
'This thing I like my sister may not do,
For she is little, and I must be kind.'

Thus boyish Will the nobler mastery learned
Where inward vision over impulse reigns,
Widening its life with separate life discerned,
A Like unlike, a Self that self restrains.

His years with others must the sweeter be
For those brief days he spent in loving me.

GEORGE ELIOT

WOMAN'S SONG

Kind kettle on my hearth
Whisper to avert God's wrath,
Scoured table, pray for me.
Jam and pickle and conserve,
Cloistered summers, named and numbered,
Me from going bad preserve;
Pray for me.

Wrung dishclout on the line
Sweeten to those nostrils fine,
Patched apron, pray for me.
Calm linen in the press,
Far-reaped meadows, ranged and fellowed,
Clothe the hour of my distress;
Pray for me.

True water from the tap
Overflow the mind's mishap,
Brown tea-pot, pray for me.
Glass and chrome and porcelain,
Earth arisen to flower a kitchen,
Shine away my shades ingrain;
Pray for me.

All things wonted, fleeting, fixed,
Stand me and myself betwixt,
Sister my mortality.
By your transience still renewed,
But more meek than mine and speechless,
In eternity's solitude,
Pray for me.

SYLVIA TOWNSEND WARNER

MARRIAGE AND DEATH

We are not dovetailed but opened to each other
So that our edges blur, and to and fro
A little wind-borne trade plies, filtering over,
Bartering our atoms when fair breezes blow.

Though, not like waters met and inter-running,
Our peoples dwell each under different sky,
Here at high, unsurveyed, dissolving frontiers
We cannot prove: 'This is you, this is I.'

Oh now in you, no more in myself only
And God, I partly live, and seem to have died,
So given up, entered and entering wholly
(To cross the threshold is to be inside),

And wonder if at last, each through each far dispersed,
We shall die easily who loved this dying first.

                                        E. J. SCOVELL

AN APRIL EPITHALAMIUM

FOR JOHN AND ANNE HUGHES

I meant to write a poem upon your wedding
Full of advice and hidden, deeper meaning.
Alas, my life has locked me out of language.
My sons skulk in their slum of drums and dinner;
Distracting wars break out on distant islands;
Rooms, uncurled in sunlight, cry for cleaning.

I'll hum some thoughts in rhythm while I'm cleaning.
Marriage, you know, is not a life-long wedding,
A launching of moony pairs to pearly islands
Where love, like light, illuminates pure meaning.
For just when truth's in sight, it's time for dinner.
Or lust (thank God) corrupts pure love of language.

Love is, of course, its appetites and language.
Nothing could be more human or more cleaning.
It seems a shame to have to think of dinner
And all the ephemeral trappings of a wedding
When what you pay for seems to cost its meaning.
Are canapes and cake somehow small islands,

Symbols in champagne of all the islands
We try to join together through our language?
John Donne was very sure about his meaning:
No John or Anne's an island. For the cleaning
up and linking up of feelings, a wedding's
A kind of causeway, then – like dinner.

O.K. A man (not John) could wed his dinner.
God help him to imagine lusty islands
Where sun and sea began life with a wedding,
Begetting – not with greedy need of language –
Greenness and creatures (winds to do the cleaning)
That ring-a-rosy in a dance of meaning,

Without which *love* might be the only meaning.
I mean, of course, that *love* and *war* and *dinner*
And *politics* and *literature* and *cleaning*
Are only words, flat atlases of islands.
While, with our mouths, we caterwaul a language,
Our eyes and bodies meet and make their wedding.

But look! I've spoiled your wedding with a meaning,
Tried to spice up with language good plain dinner.
Off to your island now! Leave me my cleaning.

ANNE STEVENSON

Faith and Religion

T HE aristocratic ladies of the Renaissance, like Elizabeth I and
Mary Sidney, Countess of Pembroke and sister of Sir Philip
Sidney, were often as well educated as their aristocratic male
counterparts. Like their menfolk these women also wrote verses to
show off their skill and learning. By the seventeenth century such
female emancipation was on the wane. That women should actually
write poetry came to be seen as a daring, rebellious, even brazen thing
to do. This strange desire could be made acceptable, however, by the
one topic on which it was considered seemly for women to write –
religion. The poems in this group naturally range widely in their
approach to questions of faith and belief. Many belong to periods
more pious and less questioning than our own.

Mary Sidney's versification of the Psalms, which she started as a
joint undertaking with her brother and completed after his early
death, is typical of the uncomplicated faith of the sixteenth century.
Anne Bradstreet, an American colonist and Puritan, wrote a similar
series called *Contemplations* which are songs of praise expressing a
simple, uplifting piety. How does her attitude to the natural world
differ from that of the English Anne Collins's similarly pietistic poem
'The Soul's Home'?

Equally devout though more complex in form, attitude and emotion
are the two poems by Christina Rossetti and Alice Meynell. 'In Sleep'
uses paradox (which is a real or seeming contradiction and is often
found in both religion and poetry) to confront the case against a loving
God. How does she do it? 'Uphill' uses a question-and-answer format
and a touch of allegory to address religious doubt. Poems which
employ dialogue as in 'Uphill' and 'In Sleep' are usually very
immediate and direct and lend themselves to dramatized reading.
Which of the two is easier to read aloud, and why?

The passionate conviction of Emily Brontë's 'No Coward Soul Is
Mine' is quite breathtaking and quite unlike the gentle piety of
Christina Rossetti. It is difficult to tell, however, if the intense faith

being expressed in this poem is an orthodox Christian one. Does her use of capital letters give us a clue? If you have read *Wuthering Heights*, can you find any clues in that novel to help you interpret the poem? Twentieth-century poets like Elizabeth Jennings find it less easy to be as certain and assertive as Romantic poets like Emily Brontë. The quiet, reasoning tone and recognition of occasional failure in 'To a Friend with a Religious Vocation' contrasts markedly with the tone of 'No Coward Soul Is Mine'. Would you say Elizabeth Jennings is any the less a believer? Are there any points in common between these two poems?

Anne Ridler's prayer to God to favour her side with victory in the Second World War, 'Now as Then', resembles 'To a Friend', in its tone of quiet reasonableness and humility. Such prayers belong to a long tradition in which poets and priests, in time of war especially, have appropriated God as their own tribal deity. Does Anne Ridler avoid this pitfall, and if so, how?

Equally quiet in tone, Sylvia Townsend Warner's 'Early One Morning' gives expression to that profound but fleeting feeling of 'otherness', that sense of disclosure that is usually subsumed under the meaning of the word 'spiritual'. This is a poem about something significant sensed but not grasped, as fleeting as dew on grass.

The following four poems seem to express something less than orthodox Christian belief. How would you describe Emily Dickinson's two short, aphoristic pieces – sceptical, agnostic, facetious, sardonic? What attitudes to faith do they express? Are these attitudes incompatible with religious belief? Compare these two brief poems with 'Drowning is not so pitiful', on page 78. What features tell you they are all by the same poet? Would you say that Edna St Vincent Millay and Stevie Smith were agnostics, atheists or critical believers? Of what are they critical – religion, man, or particular religious tenets? What effect does Stevie Smith's conversational address to her mother have on you in such a serious context?

Like 'Mother among the Dustbins', both 'Innocent Landscape' and 'Because I could not stop for Death' are imbued with a consciousness of death as the only inescapable fact of life. How do they differ in their presentation of this fact? Do they both take faith and belief for granted? Emily Dickinson's poetry always surprises us by the way it turns conventions on their heads. The simple style, ballad form and Jane Austen-like social courtesies all help to create that sense of shock. Why is this?

Finally, set to the rhythm of the hymn 'The Church's one foundation', Sylvia Townsend Warner's 'Hymn for Holy Deconsecration' bears witness to the collapse of 'mass devotion' (pun intended) in the twentieth century. How can you tell this is a humorous poem?

PSALM LXXI

Lord, on thee my trust is grounded:
Leave me not with shame confounded;
  But in Justice bring me aide.
Lett thine eare to me be bended;
Lett my life, from death defended,
  Be by thee in safety staid.

PSALM LXXII

Teach the kings sonne, who king hym selfe shall be,
  Thy judgments, Lord, thy justice make hym learn:
To rule realme as justice shall decree,
  And poore mens right in judgement to discern,
    Then fearless peace,
    With rich encrease
The mountaynes proud shall fill:
    And justice shall
    With plenty fall
On ev'ry humble hill.

                    MARY HERBERT (NÉE SIDNEY)

From CONTEMPLATIONS

2

I wist not what to wish, yet sure thought I,
If so much excellence abide below,
How excellent is He that dwells on high,
Whose power and beauty by his works we know?
Sure he is goodness, wisdom, glory, light,
That hath this under world so richly dight;
More heaven than earth was here, no winter and no night.

1 8

When I behold the heavens as in their prime,
And then the earth (though old) still clad in green,
The stones and trees, insensible of time,
Nor age nor wrinkle on their front are seen;
If winter come and greenness then do fade,
A spring returns, and they more youthful made;
But man grows old, lies down, remains where once he's laid.

2 0

Shall I then praise the heavens, the trees, the earth
Because their beauty and their strength last longer?
Shall I wish there, or never to had birth,
Because they're bigger, and their bodies stronger?
Nay, they shall darken, perish, fade and die,
And when unmade, so ever shall they lie,
But man was made for endless immortality.

ANNE BRADSTREET

THE SOUL'S HOME

Such is the force of each created thing
That it no solid happiness can bring,
Which to our minds can give contentment sound;
For, like as Noah's dove no succour found,
Till she return'd to him that sent her out,
Just so, the soul in vain may seek about
For rest or satisfaction anywhere,
Save in his presence who hath sent her here;
Yea though all earthly glories should unite
Their pomp and splendour to give such delight,
Yet could they no more sound contentment bring
Than starlight can make grass or flowers spring.

ANNE COLLINS

IN SLEEP

I dreamt (no 'dream' awake – a dream indeed)
A wrathful man was talking in the park:
'Where are the Higher Powers; who know our need
    And leave us in the dark?

There are no Higher Powers; there is no heart
In God, no love' – his oratory here,
Taking the paupers' and the cripples' part,
    Was broken by a tear.

And then it seemed that One who did create
Compassion, who alone invented pity,
Walked, as though called, in at the north-east gate,
    Out from the muttering city;

Threaded the little crowd, trod the brown grass,
Bent o'er the speaker close, saw the tear rise,
And saw Himself, as one looks in a glass,
    In those impassioned eyes.

ALICE MEYNELL

UPHILL

Does the road wind uphill all the way?
    Yes, to the very end.
Will the day's journey take the whole long day?
    From morn to night, my friend.

But is there for the night a resting-place?
    A roof for when the slow dark hours begin.
May not the darkness hide it from my face?
    You cannot miss that inn.

Shall I meet other wayfarers at night?
    Those who have gone before.
Then must I knock, or call when just in sight?
    They will not keep you standing at that door.

Shall I find comfort, travel-sore and weak?
    Of labour you shall find the sum.
Will there be beds for me and all who seek?
    Yea, beds for all who come.

CHRISTINA ROSSETTI

NO COWARD SOUL IS MINE

No coward soul is mine
No trembler in the world's storm-troubled sphere
I see Heaven's glories shine
And Faith shines equal arming me from Fear

O God within my breast
Almighty ever-present Deity
Life, that in me hast rest
As I Undying Life, have power in Thee

Vain are the thousand creeds
That move men's hearts, unutterably vain,
Worthless as withered weeds
Or idlest froth amid the boundless main

To waken doubt in one
Holding so fast by thy infinity
So surely anchored on
The steadfast rock of Immortality

With wide-embracing love
Thy spirit animates eternal years
Pervades and broods above,
Changes, sustains, dissolves, creates and rears

Though Earth and moon were gone
And suns and universes ceased to be
And thou wert left alone
Every Existence would exist in thee

There is not room for Death
Nor atom that his might could render void
Since thou art Being and Breath
And what thou art may never be destroyed.

EMILY BRONTË

TO A FRIEND WITH A RELIGIOUS VOCATION

FOR C.

Thinking of your vocation, I am filled
With thoughts of my own lack of one. I see
Within myself no wish to breed or build
Or take the three vows ringed by poverty.
      And yet I have a sense,
Vague and inchoate, with no symmetry,
Of purpose. Is it merely a pretence,

A kind of scaffolding which I erect
Half out of fear, half out of laziness?
The fitful poems come but can't protect
The empty areas of loneliness.
      You know what you must do,
So that mere breathing is a way to bless.
Dark nights, perhaps, but no grey days for you.

Your vows enfold you. I must make my own;
Now this, now that, each one empirical.
My poems move from feelings not yet known,
And when a poem is written I can feel
      A flash, a moment's peace.
The curtain will be drawn across your grille.
My silences are always enemies.

Yet with the same convictions that you have
(It is but your vocation that I lack),
I must, like you, believe in perfect love.
It is the dark, the dark that draws me back
      Into a chaos where
Vocations, visions fail, the will grows slack
And I am stunned by silence everywhere.

ELIZABETH JENNINGS

NOW AS THEN
September 1939

When under Edward or Henry the English armies
Whose battles are brocade to us and stiff in tapestries
On a green and curling sea set out for France,
The Holy Ghost moved the sails, the lance
Was hung with glory, and in all sincerity
   Poets cried 'God will grant to us the victory.'
For us, who by proxy inflicted gross oppression,
Among whom the humblest have some sins of omission,
War is not simple; in more or less degree
All are guilty, though some will suffer unjustly.
Can we say Mass to dedicate our bombs?
Yet those earlier English, for all their psalms,
Were marauders, had less provocation than we,
And the causes of war were as mixed and hard to see.
Yet since of two evils our victory would be the less,
And coming soon, leave some strength for peace,
Like Minot and the rest, groping we pray
   'Lord, turn us again, confer on us victory.'

ANNE RIDLER

'EARLY ONE MORNING . . .'

Early one morning
In a morning mist
I rose up sorrowful
And went out solitary,
And met with Christ.

I knew him instantly,
For his clothes were worn;
Carpenter's gear he carried,
And between us was growing
A winter thorn.

For leaf and blossom
It had drops of dew,
For birdsong, silence –
More lovely, more innocent
Tree never grew.

'Give me,' said I,
And my hands forlorn
Held out, 'be it only
One of these dewdrops
Hanging on the thorn.'

'Of all these dewdrops,
Hung betwixt you and me,
That must die at daybreak
I own not one of them
My own,' said he.

Hearing him speak thus,
Each dewdrop shone
Enfranchised diamond;
And with sunrising
All was gone.

SYLVIA TOWNSEND WARNER

THOSE DYING THEN

Those dying then
Knew where they went.
They went to God's right hand.
That hand is amputated now
And God cannot be found.

The abdication of belief
Makes the behaviour small;
Better an ignis fatuus
Than no illume at all.

EMILY DICKINSON

FAITH IS A FINE INVENTION

Faith is a fine invention
When gentlemen can *see*,
But *microscopes* are prudent
In an emergency.

EMILY DICKINSON

MOTHER, AMONG THE DUSTBINS

Mother, among the dustbins and the manure
I feel the measure of my humanity, an allure
As of the presence of God. I am sure

In the dustbins, in the manure, in the cat at play,
Is the presence of God, in a sure way
He moves there. Mother, what do you say?

I too have felt the presence of God in the broom
I hold, in the cobwebs in the room,
But most of all in the silence of the tomb.

Ah! but that thought that informs the hope of our kind
Is but an empty thing, what lies behind? –
Naught but the vanity of a protesting mind

That would not die. This is the thought that bounces
Within a conceited head and trounces
Inquiry. Man is most frivolous when he pronounces.

Well Mother, I shall continue to think as I do,
And I think you would be wise to do so too,
Can you question the folly of man in the creation of God?
    Who are you?

                                        STEVIE SMITH

SONNET LXVIII

TO JESUS ON HIS BIRTHDAY

For this your mother sweated in the cold,
For this you bled upon the bitter tree:
A yard of tinsel ribbon bought and sold;
A paper wreath; a day at home for me.
The merry bells ring out, the people kneel;
Up goes the man of God before the crowd;
With voice of honey and with eyes of steel
He drones your humble gospel to the proud.
Nobody listens. Less than the wind that blows
Are all your words to us you died to save.
O Prince of Peace! O Sharon's dewy Rose!
How mute you lie within your vaulted grave.
The stone the angel rolled away with tears
Is back upon your mouth these thousand years.

EDNA ST VINCENT MILLAY

INNOCENT LANDSCAPE

Here is no peace, although the air has fainted,
  And footfalls die and are buried in deep grass,
And reverential trees are softly painted
  Like saints upon an oriel of glass.

The pattern of the atmosphere is spherical,
  A bubble in the silence of the sun,
Blown thinner by the very breath of miracle
  Around a core of loud confusion.

Here is no virtue; here is nothing blessed
  Save this foredoomed suspension of the end;
Faith is the blossom, but the fruit is cursed;
  Go hence, for it is useless to pretend.

ELINOR WYLIE

BECAUSE I COULD NOT STOP FOR DEATH

Because I could not stop for Death,
He kindly stopped for me;
The carriage held but just ourselves
And Immortality.

We slowly drove, he knew no haste,
And I had put away
My labour and my leisure too,
For his civility.

We passed the school, where children strove
At wrestling in the ring;
We passed the fields of grazing grain,
We passed the setting sun.

Or rather he passed us.
The dews drew quivering and chill.
For only gossamer my gown,
My tippet only tulle.

We paused before a house that seemed
A swelling of the ground;
The roof was scarcely visible,
The cornice but a mound.

Since then 'tis centuries; but each
Feels shorter than the day
I first surmised the horses' heads
Were toward eternity.

EMILY DICKINSON

HYMN FOR HOLY DECONSECRATION

The Church's own detergent
Infallibly prevails
When Industry grows urgent
And mass devotion fails.
A single application
Removes th'inherent soil
Of previous consecration –
No need to scrub or boil.

O mystical emulsion!
O supervenient Tide!
It ousts the harsh compulsion
Of rape or suicide.
Outmoding all exertion
With candle, bell and book,
Its bubbling bland coercion
Pervades each hallowed nook.

Unchanged in outward seeming
But inwardly renewed,
Behold the fabric gleaming,
Disblest and disempewed!
Released from every rubric,
From every grace set free,
It soars as though of new brick
To Secularity.

Today, though few in number
In purpose firmly shod,
We join to disencumber
This edifice of God.
Convinced th'Eternal Father
Who chose this His abode
By now would really rather
Move further up the road.
SYLVIA TOWNSEND WARNER

Death

D EATH is today a taboo subject, which it certainly wasn't in
the past. You probably find it a morbid topic, but like the
weather, it is compulsory sooner or later for all of us.
Perhaps because of this, death has been a traditional theme for poets
through the centuries. Among male poets the theme of death, when
not linked to considerations of religious faith, has often been handled
in terms of the Latin poet's 'carpe diem', expressed most memorably
in English by the seventeenth-century poet Robert Herrick, as
'Gather ye rosebuds while ye may'. In other words, make merry now
for tomorrow we shall die. This hedonistic attitude is not one that
women poets seem interested in, perhaps because in poetry it was
often a prelude to an attempt at seduction.

The women poets in this section bring a fresh and, in some cases,
quite extraordinary slant to the topic. The approach of Margaret,
Duchess of Newcastle, to the subject in 'Nature's Cook' is very
unusual, if not shocking. She writes like a Metaphysical poet, using
imagery from a most unexpected source – the culinary arts – to
itemize different ways of dying. Look at the form (heroic couplet) and
the movement (iambic pentameter) of the poem. How do they prevent
the poem from becoming simply morbid? What do you think of such a
poem? Is it amusing, clever, gruesome, unpleasant?

Equally extraordinary and perhaps even more fantastic is Michael
Field's sonnet 'The Mummy Invokes His Soul'. Though its setting is
in the tomb and its title leads us to expect matters of spiritual moment,
this is a poem that is less concerned with metaphysics than with the
physical side of love. What details suggest that the mummy's interest
lies in resurrecting its past sexual pleasures? What do you think of
such poems? Are they amusing, clever, gruesome, unpleasant, witty?

Just as surprising, though in an entirely different way, is Emily
Dickinson's 'I heard a fly buzz when I died', in which the poet
describes her own deathbed scene and the very instant of her
extinction. Clearly it is not possible for any of us to know what those

final few moments will be like. What is her purpose, then, in attempting to imagine them so closely? Is she trying to say something about the nature of each individual death or something about the necessity of attendant religious rites, or both? What effect does the appearance of so mundane and undignified a thing as a fly have on you in such a solemn context? How would you describe this poem – strange, unnerving, realistic?

Like 'I heard a fly buzz', 'Rembrandt's Late Self-Portraits' and 'Castle Wood' seem to entertain no fear of death. Discuss the reasons for this. Look carefully at the style and movement of Elizabeth Jennings's poem. Although it uses a rhyme scheme, this is barely noticeable. Why is this so? Try reading this poem aloud to a partner or a group. What do you notice? How does it compare with a reading aloud of 'Castle Wood' with its ballad-like form?

Two other poems which betray no fear of death are 'First Death in Nova Scotia' and 'Tropical Death'. They are also similar in that climate or geographical latitude seems to play an important part in each poem. Elizabeth Bishop's strange story is told from the point of view of a small child. What details in the poem suggest a child's limited view? This poem is written in 'free verse'. In dispensing with the pattern of rhyme, the poet has adopted a pattern of colours to give shape to the experience she is describing. How effective would you say they are?

It seems odd in the context to describe Grace Nichols's West Indian response to death as exhilarating. Do you think this is an appropriate word and, if so, why? What effect does ending the poem with the word 'yes' have on you?

Death is not normally sought so defiantly as it is in Emily Brontë's poem. What is more usual in poetry is the acute sense of loss expressed in Christina Rossetti's 'Dirge' and Edna St Vincent Millay's 'Elegy – Memorial to D.C.' What aspect of her friend's death does Millay lament? Can you suggest why there is a sudden break in the first line of the second verse? Rossetti's 'Dirge' laments not so much the death of the person addressed as the bad timing of it. Why does the natural imagery she employs make us think of Christ? The poem's title, which is a song sung at a burial, tells us that the poem has musical qualities. Poetic 'songs' aspire to be light, lyrical and more interested in emotion than idea. Is 'Dirge' a good example of the genre?

There is, of course, a natural human tendency to want to postpone death as long as possible, which Patricia Beer and Emily Dickinson give expression to in 'Abbey Tomb' and 'Drowning is not so pitiful'. As always, Emily Dickinson surprises us. Her poem is clearly ironic. What is irony? Discuss its purpose in this poem. How does the tragic story told in 'Abbey Tomb' turn out to be ironic?

Finally on a more optimistic note, Anne Ridler's 'Nothing Is Lost' and Christina Rossetti's 'Remember' are attempts by the poets to reconcile themselves and us to the finality of death. What are their arguments? Discuss how convincing you find them. Christina Rossetti's sonnet has always been popular with anthologists. Can you suggest why this might be?

NATURE'S COOK

Death is the cook of nature and we find
Creatures drest several ways to please her mind.
Some Death doth roast with fevers burning hot,
And some he boils with dropsies in a pot,
Some are consumed for jelly by degrees,
And some with ulcers, gravy out to squeeze;
Some, as with herbs, he stuffs with gouts and pains,
Others for tender meat he hangs in chains;
Some in the sea he pickles up to keep,
Others he, as soused brawn, in wine doth steep;
Some flesh and bones he with the Pox chops small,
And doth a French fricassee make withall;
Some on grid-irons of calentures are broiled,
And some are trodden down, and so quite spoiled.
But some are baked, when smothered they do die,
Some meat he doth by hectick fevers fry;
In sweat sometimes he stews with savory smell
An hodge-podge of diseases he likes well;
Some brains he dresseth with apoplexy,
Or Sawce of *megrims*, swimming plenteously;
And tongues he dries with smoak from stomachs ill,
Which, as the second course he sends up still;
Throats he doth cut, blood puddings for to make,
And puts them in the guts, which cholicks rack;
Some hunted are by him for deer, that's red,
And some as stall-fed oxen knocked o' th' head;
Some singed and scald for bacon, seem most rare,
When with salt rheum and phlegm they powdered are.

MARGARET CAVENDISH, DUCHESS OF NEWCASTLE

THE MUMMY INVOKES HIS SOUL

Down to me quickly, down! I am such dust,
Baked, pressed together; let my flesh be fanned
With thy fresh breath: come from thy reedy land
Voiceful with birds; divert me, for I lust
To break, to crumble – prick with pores this crust!
And fall apart delicious, loosening sand.
Oh, joy, I feel thy breath, I feel thy hand
That searches for my heart, and trembles just
Where once it beat. How light thy touch, thy frame!
Surely thou perchest on the summer trees. . .
And the garden that we loved? Soul, take thine ease,
I am content, so thou enjoy the same
Sweet terraces and founts, content, for thee,
To burn in this immense torpidity.

MICHAEL FIELD

I HEARD A FLY BUZZ WHEN I DIED

I heard a fly buzz when I died;
The stillness in the room
Was like the stillness in the air
Between the heaves of storm.

The eyes around had wrung them dry,
And breaths were gathering firm
For that last onset, when the king be
Witnessed in the room.

I willed my keepsakes, signed away
What portion of me be
Assignable – and then it was
There interposed a fly,

With blue, uncertain, stumbling buzz,
Between the light and me;
And then the windows failed, and then
I could not seem to see.

EMILY DICKINSON

REMBRANDT'S LATE SELF-PORTRAITS

You are confronted with yourself. Each year
The pouches fill, the skin is uglier.
You give it all unflinchingly. You stare
Into yourself, beyond. Your brush's care
Runs with self-knowledge. Here

Is a humility at one with craft.
There is no arrogance. Pride is apart
From this self-scrutiny. You make light drift
The way you want. Your face is bruised and hurt
But there is still love left.

Love of the art and others. To the last
Experiment went on. You stared beyond
Your age, the times. You also plucked the past
And tempered it. Self-portraits understand,
And old age can divest,

With truthful changes, us of fear of death.
Look, a new anguish. There, the bloated nose,
The sadness and the joy. To paint's to breathe,
And all the darknesses are dared. You chose
What each must reckon with.

ELIZABETH JENNINGS

CASTLE WOOD

The day is done, the winter sun
Is setting in its sullen sky;
And drear the course that has been run,
And dim the hearts that slowly die.

No star will light my coming night;
No morn of hope for me will shine;
I mourn not heaven would blast my sight,
And I never longed for ways divine.

Through Life's hard Task I did not ask
Celestial aid, celestial cheer;
I saw my fate without its mask,
And met it too without a tear.

The grief that pressed this living breast
Was heavier far than earth can be;
And who would dread eternal rest
When labour's hire was agony?

Dark falls the fear of this despair
On spirits born for happiness;
But I was bred the mate of care,
The foster-child of sore distress.

No sighs for me, no sympathy,
No wish to keep my soul below;
The heart is dead since infancy,
Unwept for let the body go.

EMILY BRONTË

FIRST DEATH IN NOVA SCOTIA

In the cold, cold parlour
my mother laid out Arthur
beneath the chromographs:
Edward, Prince of Wales,
with Princess Alexandra,
and King George with Queen Mary.
Below them on the table
stood a stuffed loon
shot and stuffed by Uncle
Arthur, Arthur's father.

Since Uncle Arthur fired
a bullet into him,
he hadn't said a word.
He kept his own counsel
on his white, frozen lake,
the marble-topped table.

His breast was deep and white,
cold and caressable;
his eyes were red glass,
much to be desired.

'Come,' said my mother,
'Come and say goodbye
to your little cousin Arthur.'
I was lifted up and given
one lily of the valley
to put in Arthur's hand.
Arthur's coffin was
a little frosted cake,
and the red-eyed loon eyed it
from his white, frozen lake.

Arthur was very small.
He was all white, like a doll
that hadn't been painted yet.
Jack Frost had started to paint him
the way he always painted
the Maple Leaf (Forever).
He had just begun on his hair,
a few red strokes, and then
Jack Frost had dropped the brush
and left him white, forever.

The gracious royal couples
were warm in red and ermine;
their feet were well wrapped up
in the ladies' ermine trains.
They invited Arthur to be
the smallest page at court.
But how could Arthur go,
clutching his tiny lily,
with his eyes shut up so tight
and the roads deep in snow?

ELIZABETH BISHOP

TROPICAL DEATH

The fat black woman want
a brilliant tropical death
not a cold sojourn
in some North Europe far/forlorn

The fat black woman want
some heat/hibiscus at her feet
blue sea dress
to wrap her neat

The fat black woman want
some bawl
no quiet jerk tear wiping
a polite hearse withdrawal

The fat black woman want
all her dead rights
first night
third night
nine night
all the sleepless droning
red-eyed wake nights

In the heart
of her mother's sweetbreast
In the shade
of the sun leaf's cool bless
In the bloom
of her people's bloodrest

the fat black woman want
a brilliant tropical death yes

GRACE NICHOLS

MEMORIAL TO D.C.
(VASSAR COLLEGE, 1918)

O' loveliest throat of all sweet throats,
Where now no more the music is,
With hands that wrote you little notes
I write you little elegies!

ELEGY

Let them bury your big eyes
In the secret earth securely,
Your thin fingers, and your fair,
Soft, indefinite-coloured hair –
All of these in some way, surely,
From the secret earth shall rise;
Not for these I sit and stare,
Broken and bereft completely:
Your young flesh that sat so neatly
On your little bones so sweetly
Blossom in the air.

But your voice . . . never the rushing
Of a river underground,
Not the rising of the wind
In the trees before the rain,
Not the woodcock's watery call,
Not the note the white-throat utters,
Not the feet of children pushing
Yellow leaves along the gutters
In the blue and bitter fall,
Shall content my musing mind
For the beauty of that sound
That in no new way at all
Ever will be heard again.

Sweetly through the sappy stalk
Of the vigorous weed,
Holding all it held before,
Cherished by the faithful sun,
On and on eternally
Shall your altered fluid run,
Bud and bloom and go to seed;
But your singing days are done;
But the music of your talk
Never shall the chemistry
Of the secret earth restore.
All your lovely words are spoken.
Once the ivory box is broken
Beats the golden bird no more.

EDNA ST VINCENT MILLAY

A DIRGE

Why were you born when the snow was falling?
You should have come to the cuckoo's calling,
Or when grapes are green in the cluster,
Or at least when lithe swallows muster
        For their far off flying
        From summer dying.

Why did you die when the lambs were cropping?
You should have died at the apples' dropping,
When the grasshopper comes to trouble,
And the wheat-fields are sodden stubble,
        And all winds go sighing
        For sweet things dying.

CHRISTINA ROSSETTI

ABBEY TOMB

I told them not to ring the bells
The night the Vikings came
Out of the sea and passed us by.
The fog was thick as cream
And in the abbey we stood still
As if our breath might blare
Or pulses rattle if we once
Stopped staring at the door.

Through the walls and through the fog
We heard them passing by.
The deafer monks thanked God too soon
And later only I
Could catch the sound of prowling men
Still present in the hills
So everybody else agreed
To ring the abbey bells.

And even while the final clang
Still snored upon the air,
And while the ringers joked their way
Down round the spiral stair,
Before the spit of fervent prayer
Had dried into the stone
The raiders came back through the fog
And killed us one by one.

Father Abbot at the altar
Lay back with his knees
Doubled under him, caught napping
In the act of praise.
Brother John lay unresponsive
In the warming room.
The spiders came out for the heat
And then the rats for him.

Under the level of the sheep
Who graze here all the time
We lie now, under tourists' feet
Who in good weather come.
I told them not to ring the bells
But centuries of rain
And blustering have made their tombs
Look just as right as mine.

PATRICIA BEER

DROWNING IS NOT SO PITIFUL

Drowning is not so pitiful
As the attempt to rise.
Three times, 'tis said, a sinking man
Comes up to face the skies,
And then declines forever
To that abhorred abode,
Where hope and he part company –
For he is grasped of God.
The Maker's cordial visage,
However good to see,
Is shunned, we must admit it,
Like an adversity.

EMILY DICKINSON

NOTHING IS LOST

Nothing is lost.
We are too sad to know that, or too blind;
Only in visited moments do we understand:
It is not that the dead return –
They are about us always, though unguessed.

This pencilled Latin verse
You dying wrote me, ten years past and more,
Brings you as much alive to me as the self you wrote it for,
Dear father, as I read your words
With no word but Alas.

Lines in a letter, lines in a face
Are faithful currents of life: the boy has written
His parents across his forehead, and as we burn
Our bodies up each seven years,
His own past self has left no plainer trace.

Nothing dies.
The cells pass on their secrets, we betray them
Unknowingly: in a freckle, in the way
We walk, recall some ancestor,
And Adam in the colour of our eyes.

Yes, on the face of the new born,
Before the soul has taken full possession,
There pass, as over a screen, in succession
   The images of other beings:
      Face after face looks out, and then is gone.

      Nothing is lost, for all in love survive.
I lay my cheek against his sleeping limbs
To feel if he is warm, and touch in him
   Those children whom no shawl could warm,
      No arms, no grief, no longing could revive.

      Thus what we see, or know,
Is only a tiny portion, at the best,
Of the life in which we share; an iceberg's crest
   Our sunlit present, our partial sense,
      With deep supporting multitudes below.

ANNE RIDLER

REMEMBER

Remember me when I am gone away,
Gone far away into the silent land;
When you can no more hold me by the hand,
Nor I half turn to go, yet turning stay.
Remember me when no more day by day
You tell me of our future that you planned:
Only remember me; you understand
It will be late to counsel then or pray.
Yet if you should forget me for a while
And afterwards remember, do not grieve:
For if the darkness and corruption leave
A vestige of the thoughts that once I had,
Better by far you should forget and smile
Than that you should remember and be sad.

CHRISTINA ROSSETTI

War

U NTIL the twentieth century, war was an experience from
which the vast mass of women were excluded. Their
function was to react as mothers, wives, sisters and lovers to
the mutilation and death that war inflicted on men close to them, in
their families or communities. During the First World War, and more
especially the Second World War, large numbers of women played a
more active role, but not as combatants. They did, however, make a
genuine contribution to the war effort and the defence of their
country. For example, they worked in munitions factories, as nurses at
the Front, as anti-aircraft gunners and as ambulance drivers during
the Blitz. Because the Second World War was such a total war,
involving the bombardment of the home front, and because of the
mass media (and newsreel film especially), women too grew to
know the dangers and stresses that their men endured in Europe and
North Africa.

When wars were confined to distant battlefields it was easy for both
men and women to write recruiting songs and verses that ignored the
realities for those who actually had to do the fighting. Julia Ward
Howe's 'Battle Hymn of the Republic' was published in 1862 in the
first year of the American Civil War. In assuming that her side in the
war is doing God's work, she resembles Anne Ridler in 'Now As
Then' (on page 60), but the imagery, tone and rhythm of the two
poems are vastly different. Which of them makes the most immediate
impression on you and why? (Remember, this need not be the better
poem.)

Jessie Pope's 'The Beau Ideal', written during the First World War,
is another recruiting effort composed for a newspaper. How would
you describe the tone of these two recruiting pieces – rousing, stirring,
self-righteous? Do you agree with the view that 'The Beau Ideal' is
inadvertently humorous? Or is it simply in bad taste?

Alice Dunbar Nelson, a black American journalist and short-story
writer who wrote few poems, was deeply moved by reports of the
carnage in Flanders. Compare 'The Beau Ideal' and 'I Sit and Sew',
in both of which the woman is far distant from the scenes of suffering.

Each poem is built on a series of contrasts. What are they in each poem and how effective are they?

'Summer in England 1914' and 'From A Letter to America on a Visit to Sussex: Spring 1942' also each develop a series of contrasts. What effect does the exquisitely beautiful imagery of Alice Meynell's poem have on our perception of the horrors she also records? Does it reinforce the suffering or diminish it? In what way is this also a religious poem? And as such, how does it compare with 'Battle Hymn'? Frances Cornford's 'Letter 1942' is about the unexpected contrasts that wartime throws up. What would you say was the point of the uneven line lengths in this poem? Is it to stress the poem's theme of unexpectedness? Emily Brontë's 'Why Ask to Know the Date – the Clime?' makes plain the universal affliction that is war whenever and wherever it is fought. Without any personal experience of military conflict, Emily Brontë seemed to understand perfectly the civil effects of war, even down to the devastation of crops and the disruption of the agricultural year.

In contrast to the universalizing and generalizing approach of the three preceding poets, Eleanor Farjeon, Teresa Hooley and Pamela Holmes express a purely personal perspective in response to war. They explore their own particular feelings or their own individual misfortune. 'Easter Monday: in memoriam E.T.' expresses in a series of subtle ironies Eleanor Farjeon's grief on the death in 1917 of the man she loved, fellow poet Edward Thomas. The cruel irony of his abrupt destruction in the midst of the burgeoning renewal of the natural world he so delighted in points up the poem's poignancy. The conversational tone and specificity of vocabulary like 'munch' make for an immediacy which ironically belies the poem's subject. Can you suggest a reason for the studious avoidance of rhyme in a poem whose form and length lead us to believe that it is a sonnet? Look closely at the punctuation of 'A War Film'. What effects do you think Teresa Hooley seeks to convey by means of her unfinished sentences and by the distinctive punctuation of lines 12 and 13 of the third stanza?

Except for a few key words, the language of Pamela Holmes's poem 'Missing, Presumed Killed' is monosyllabic and plain. How does this affect your perception of her tragedy? Does it make her grief more accessible and more vivid, or more flat and ordinary? She is one of the few poets in this section to write from personal experience of loss. She was only 20 when her husband was killed and she wrote this poem. Do you find it ends hopefully? Compare it with Eleanor Farjeon's 'Easter Monday'. Which is the better poem?

The last three poems are about children caught up in other people's wars. 'A Son' records one of the many poignantly sad incidents that war inflicts on individuals however innocent and defenceless. It resembles Wordsworth's 'Michael' in its bleak picture of a barren life redeemed by maternity only to be shattered by a bomb. This is a starkly moving poem until the end. What would you say is wrong with the last line? Does it affect your response to the rest of the poem? 'A War Film', like 'Missing, Presumed Killed' and 'I Sit and Sew', is written in the first person, which can be a powerful way of expressing feelings. 'A Son' is told in the third person by the poet as storyteller about a couple known to her. How does Lilian Bowes Lyon help us share the feelings of her inarticulate couple?

Two poems about the experience of evacuation during the Second World War, when large numbers of city children were uprooted for their own safety and sent to the country without their mothers, show that children's responses to such traumatic experiences differed vastly. How do these two poems compare? What are the advantages both poets see embodied by life in the countryside? The loneliness of unaccustomed surroundings drives the child in 'Evacuee' to attempt to run away. Do you think the poet's attitude in this poem is one of pity and sympathy? The language of 'The Evacuees' is full of metaphors from human life applied to inanimate things, like 'grass . . . combed . . . coiffed', 'smile of eggs' and 'stare of cheeses'. What do you think Freda Laughton is trying to convey by such imagery?

BATTLE HYMN OF THE REPUBLIC

Mine eyes have seen the glory of the coming of the Lord;
He is trampling out the vintage where the grapes of wrath are stored;
He hath loosed the fateful lightning of His terrible, swift sword;
 His truth is marching on.

I have seen Him in the watch-fires of a hundred circling camps;
They have builded Him an altar in the evening dews and damps;
I can read His righteous sentence by the dim and flaring lamps;
 His day is marching on.

I have read a fiery gospel, writ in burnished rows of steel:
'As ye deal with my contemners, so with you my grace shall deal;
Let the Hero, born of woman, crush the serpent with his heel,
 Since God is marching on.'

He has sounded forth the trumpet that shall never call retreat;
He is sifting out the hearts of men before His judgement-seat:
Oh, be swift, my soul, to answer Him! be jubilant, my feet!
 Our God is marching on.

In the beauty of the lilies Christ was born across the sea,
With a glory in His bosom that transfigures you and me:
As He died to make men holy, let us die to make men free,
 While God is marching on.

JULIA WARD HOWE

THE BEAU IDEAL

Since Rose a classic taste possessed,
    It naturally follows
Her girlish fancy was obsessed
    By Belvidere Apollos.
And when she dreamed about a mate,
    If any hoped to suit, he
Must in his person illustrate
    A type of manly beauty.

He must be physically fit,
    A graceful, stalwart figure,
Of iron and elastic knit
    And full of verve and vigour.
Enough! I've made the bias plain
    That warped her heart and thrilled it.
It was a maggot of her brain
    And Germany has killed it.

To-day, the sound in wind and limb
    Don't flutter Rose one tittle.
Her maiden ardour cleaves to him
    Who's proved that he is brittle,
Whose healing cicatrices show
    The colours of a prism,
Whose back is bent into a bow
    By Flanders rheumatism.

The lad who troth with Rose would plight
    Nor apprehend rejection,
Must be in shabby khaki dight
    To compass her affection.
Who buys her an engagement ring
    And finds her kind and kissing,
Must have one member in a sling
    Or, preferably, missing.

JESSIE POPE

I SIT AND SEW

I sit and sew – a useless task it seems,
My hands grown tired, my head weighed down with dreams –
The panoply of war, the material tread of men,
Grim-faced, stern-eyed, gazing beyond the ken
Of lesser souls, whose eyes have not seen Death,
Nor learned to hold their lives but as a breath –
But – I must sit and sew.

I sit and sew – my heart aches with desire –
That pageant terrible, that fiercely pouring fire
On wasted fields, and writhing grotesque things
Once men. My soul in pity flings
Appealing cries, yearning only to go
There in that holocaust of hell, those fields of woe –
But – I must sit and sew.

The little useless seam, the idle patch;
Why dream I here beneath my homely thatch,
When there they lie in sodden mud and rain,
Pitifully calling me, the quick ones and the slain!
You need me, Christ! It is no roseate dream
That beckons me – this pretty futile seam,
It stifles me – God, must I sit and sew?

ALICE DUNBAR NELSON

SUMMER IN ENGLAND, 1914

On London fell a clearer light;
   Caressing pencils of the sun
Defined the distances, the white
   Houses transfigured one by one,
The 'long, unlovely street' impearled.
O what a sky has walked the world!

Most happy year! And out of town
   The hay was prosperous, and the wheat;
The silken harvest climbed the down:
   Moon after moon was heavenly-sweet.
Stroking the bread within the sheaves,
Looking 'twixt apples and their leaves.

And while this rose made round her cup,
   The armies died convulsed. And when
This chaste young silver sun went up
   Softly, a thousand shattered men,
One wet corruption, heaped the plain,
After a league-long throb of pain.

Flower following tender flower; and birds,
   And berries; and benignant skies
Made thrive the serried flocks and herds –
   Yonder are men shot through the eyes.
     Love, hide thy face
From man's unpardonable race.

Who said, 'No man hath greater love than this,
   To die to serve his friend'?
So these have loved us all unto the end.
   Chide thou no more, O thou unsacrificed!
The soldier dying dies upon a kiss,
   The very kiss of Christ.

ALICE MEYNELL

FROM A LETTER TO AMERICA
ON A VISIT TO SUSSEX:
SPRING 1942

How simply violent things
Happen, is strange.
How strange it was to see
In the soft Cambridge sky our Squadron's wings,
And hear the huge hum in the familiar grey.
And it was odd today
On Ashdown Forest that will never change,
To find a gunner in the gorse, flung down,
Well-camouflaged, and bored and lion-brown.
A little further by those twisted trees
(As if it rose on humped preposterous seas
Out of a Book of Hours) up a bank
Like a large dragon, purposeful though drunk,
Heavily lolloped, swayed and sunk,
A tank.
All this because manoeuvres had begun.
But now, but soon,
At home on any usual afternoon,
High overhead
May come the Erinyes winging.
Or here the boy may lie beside his gun,
His mud-brown tunic gently staining red,
While larks get on with their old job of singing.

FRANCES CORNFORD

From WHY ASK TO KNOW THE DATE –
THE CLIME?

Why ask to know the date – the clime?
More than mere words they cannot be:
Men knelt to God and worshipped crime,
And crushed the helpless, even as we.

But they had learnt, from length of strife
Of civil war and anarchy,
To laugh at death and look on life
With somewhat lighter sympathy.

It was the autumn of the year,
The time to labouring peasants dear;
Week after week, from noon to noon,
September shone as bright as June –
Still, never hand a sickle held;
The crops were garnered in the field –
Trod out and ground by horses' feet
While every ear was milky sweet;
And kneaded on the threshing-floor
With mire of tears and human gore.
Some said they thought that heaven's pure rain
Would hardly bless those fields again:
No so – the all-benignant skies
Rebuked that fear of famished eyes –
July passed on with showers and dew,
And August glowed in showerless blue;
No harvest time could be more fair
Had harvest fruits but ripened there.

EMILY BRONTË

EASTER MONDAY:
IN MEMORIAM E.T.

In the last letter that I had from France
You thanked me for the silver Easter egg
Which I had hidden in the box of apples
You liked to munch beyond all other fruit.
You found the egg the Monday before Easter
And said, 'I will praise Easter Monday now –
It was such a lovely morning.' Then you spoke
Of the coming battle and said 'This is the eve.
Goodbye. And may I have a letter soon.'

That Easter Monday was a day for praise,
It was such a lovely morning. In our garden
We sowed our earliest seeds, and in the orchard
The apple-bud was ripe. It was the eve.
There are three letters that you will not get.

ELEANOR FARJEON

A WAR FILM

I saw,
With a catch of the breath and the heart's uplifting,
Sorrow and pride,
   The 'week's great draw' –
The Mons Retreat;
The 'Old Contemptibles' who fought, and died,
The horror and the anguish and the glory.

As in a dream,
Still hearing machine-guns rattle and shells scream,
I came out into the street.
When the day was done,
My little son
Wondered at bath-time why I kissed him so,
Naked upon my knee.
How could he know
The sudden terror that assaulted me? . . .
The body I had borne
Nine moons beneath my heart,
A part of me . . .
If, someday,
It should be taken away
To war. Tortured. Torn.
Slain.
Rotting in No Man's Land, out in the rain –
My little son . . .
Yet all those men had mothers, every one.

How should he know
Why I kissed and kissed and kissed him, crooning his name?
He thought that I was daft.
He thought it was a game,
And laughed, and laughed.

TERESA HOOLEY

MISSING, PRESUMED KILLED

There is no cross to mark
The place he lies,
And no man shared his dark Gethsemane,
Or, witnessing that simple sacrifice,
Brought word to me.

There is no grave for him;
The mourning heart
Knows not the destination of its prayer,
Save that he is anonymous, apart,
Sleeping out there.

But though strict earth may keep
Her secret well,
She cannot claim his immortality;
Safe from that darkness whence he fell,
He comes to me.

PAMELA HOLMES

A SON

A middle-aged farm-labourer lived here,
And loved his wife; paid rent to hard eternity
Six barren years, till thorn-tree-blessed she bore
A son with a bird's glint, and wheat-straw hair.
Sweet life! Yet neither boasted.
The boy was a tassel flown by gaunt serenity,
Hedge banner in the September of the War.

A jettisoned bomb fell; at noonday there,
Where take my dusty oath a cottage stood.
Great with unspendable centuries of maternity,
'At least he had struck seven,' she said, 'this year –'
Of different grace; of blood.
The man looks bent; yet neither girds at God,
Remembering it was beautiful while it lasted.

LILIAN BOWES LYON

EVACUEE

The slum had been his home since he was born;
And then war came, and he was rudely torn
From all he'd ever known; and with his case
Of mean necessities, brought to a place
Of silences and space; just boom of sea
And sough of wind; small wonder then that he
Crept out one night to seek his sordid slum,
And thought to find his way. By dawn he'd come
A few short miles; and cattle in their herds
Gazed limpidly as he trudged by, and birds
Just stirring in first light, awoke to hear
His lonely sobbing, born of abject fear
Of sea and hills and sky; of silent night
Unbroken by the sound of shout and fight.

EDITH PICKTHALL

THE EVACUEES

There is no sound of guns here, nor echo of guns.
The spasm of bombs has dissolved
Into the determination of the tractor.

Our music now is the rasp of the corncrake
And the wedge-shaped call of the cuckoo
Above leaves tranced in the lap of summer.

We have discovered the grass, curled in the ditches.
We have combed it with rakes in the hayfields,
And coiffed it in lion-coloured stacks.

We have stroked milk, warm and gentle from the cow,
The placid primitive milk, before bottles
Sterilise its mild wonder.

We have met the bland smile of eggs in a willow-basket;
Returned the stolid stare of cheeses ripening on the shelf;
Warmed ourselves at the smell of baking bread.

We have seen food, the sacrament of life,
Not emasculate and defunct upon dishes, but alive,
Springing from the earth after the discipline of the plough.

FREDA LAUGHTON

Politics and Social Protest

I T WAS not until the twentieth century that women in Britain won the right to vote and so became officially and formally involved in political actions. This had not, however, prevented women in earlier times from agitating for women's suffrage and for other worthy political causes. While prison reformers like Elizabeth Fry in the early nineteenth century and nursing pioneers like Florence Nightingale later in the century worked tirelessly for their respective good causes, women poets wrote about social conditions and political issues and thereby publicized what they too felt strongly about.

Among women poets Elizabeth Barrett Browning was most energetic in exercising her talent on behalf of political causes. She wrote in support of Italian emancipation from Austrian rule and in vilification of the industrial exploitation of children in England. 'The Cry of the Children' is a direct attack on the use of child labour in coal mines. Mary Barber's poem 'On Seeing an Officer's Widow Distracted' is also a response to real conditions of suffering, in this case madness caused by the government's failure to pay an officer's widow her rightful pension. Which of the following words do you think describes these two poems – outrage, anger, compassion, horror, fear?

The next two poems – 'Kitchenette Building' and 'The Choosing' – look at social conditions and at attitudes in a subtle way through the choices people, especially women, make. How free does Gwendolyn Brooks, a black American poet, suggest these are in 'Kitchenette Building'? Why have the later lives of such equally placed primary-school girls diverged so widely in Liz Lochhead's 'The Choosing'? How have their respective choices been made?

Not all political poems are as overt as the first two in this section. The issue of women's suffrage is taken up in an oblique and subtle way by Alice Meynell in 'A Father of Women' published in 1917, a year before the vote was finally granted (to women of 30 and over). It is an unusual mix of war poem, tribute to her own father and political protest. Her commitment to political justice for women does not allow her to minimize the unbearably cruel ironies of the historical situation and the high price finally paid by the fathers and the sons. Prophetically, she connects the carnage of the millions of sons in Flanders with the eventual need to concede the franchise to the daughters (who proved their worth by working in place of the absent and the dead). Would you agree that the poem's final effect is one of starkness, even harshness? How is such an effect conveyed given the poem's studiedly polished style?

'The Cry of the Children' was about children working down coal mines. The world of work figures also in 'The Woman's Labour, an epistle' by the eighteenth-century peasant-poet Mary Collier and in 'Insec' Lesson' by a contemporary West Indian poet, Valerie Bloom. At first sight, neither of these poems seems as obviously political as 'The Cry of the Children', yet both have political/social points to make but do so indirectly. Both are celebratory poems. What is it they are paying tribute to? Mary Collier's poem reminds us of pre-industrial conditions on the land for the poor. 'The Woman's Labour, an epistle' is a riposte to one Stephen Duck, whose poem 'The Thresher's Labour', which argued that working men had harder labours to perform than Hercules, also took women to task. Mary Collier's life as agricultural labourer, laundress and domestic servant equipped her to reply with a realistic picture of women's unequal lot in fields and house. In what ways is her poem more sophisticated than her disclaimer in line 7 would suggest? Look at both her style and argument. In what ways does Valerie Bloom use the ant as a symbol? What is the point of dialect in this poem? Is it a way of suggesting the poet's apparent puzzlement?

The next three poems, all from the nineteenth century, are about the dire poverty of that age and the suffering and deprivation it caused, but they each approach the subject quite differently. Mary Lamb's childlike squib contrasts the need to read and feed one's mind with the need to eat. How and why is this an ironic poem? The excerpt from Christina Rossetti's 'A Royal Princess' cloaks its critique of Victorian attitudes to the poor and to women in a fairy tale-type narrative. How is it that the heroine's action at the end can be described as both a life and a death? Dora Greenwell on the other hand tells the story of one dying man whose life has been unimaginably restricted. What would you say are the emotions expressed in 'When the Night and Morning Meet' – sorrow, dismay, hopelessness? Like many poems in this anthology, this one could have been included in another section. Which other section could that be?

Which of these three poems do you find the most affecting and why?

As social conditions for the mass of the people have improved during this century and especially since the Second World War, and as women's rights have been recognized in statute, our ideas of what is 'political' have shifted ground. We end this section with three poems that would not, until recently, have been thought to be expressing political concerns.

The extract from George Eliot's 'A Minor Prophet' describes a type of radical visionary it is not unusual to find today, a type not restricted to religious bigotry. What phrases and ideas make one think this is a humorous portrait? What kind of humour is expressed here? Is it satirical and cruel or a more gentle, humane poking fun at eccentricity? Do you agree with George Eliot's critique of this man's views? What, for her, gives life its savour and why? Why should this poem about an eccentric with a Utopian vision be included in a section on politics?

A concern among women for the welfare of animals antedates the modern animal rights and 'Green' movements, and even the rise of anti-vivisectionism in the past century. 'Lucky' is in the same tradition as the Duchess of Newcastle's 'The Hunting of the Hare' which is an early and spirited attack on blood sports. The first part of the poem describes the hunt from the terrified hare's point of view. How effectively does she convey this? The final 20 lines of the poem examine the false arguments and ironic rationalizations men employ to justify their gory pleasure. Why are their self-justifications ironic?

From THE CRY OF THE CHILDREN

φεῦ, φεῦ, τι προσδερκεσθε
μ'ομμασιν, τεκνα.

Euripides, *Medea*

Do ye hear the children weeping, O my brothers,
        Ere the sorrow comes with years?
They are leaning their young heads against their mothers, –
        And *that* cannot stop their tears.
The young lambs are bleating in the meadows;
        The young birds are chirping in the nest;
The young fawns are playing with the shadows;
        The young flowers are blowing toward the west –
But the young, young children, O my brothers,
        They are weeping bitterly! –
They are weeping in the playtime of the others,
        In the country of the free.

Do you question the young children in their sorrow,
        Why their tears are falling so? –
The old man may weep for his to-morrow
        Which is lost in Long Ago –
The old tree is leafless in the forest –
        The old year is ending in the frost –
The old wound, if stricken, is the sorest –
        The old hope is hardest to be lost:
But the young, young children, O my brothers,
        Do you ask them why they stand
Weeping sore before the bosoms of their mothers,
        In our happy Fatherland?

. . . .
.

Alas, the wretched children! they are seeking
      Death in life; as best to have!
They are binding up their hearts away from breaking,
      With a cerement from the grave.
Go out, children, from the mine and from the city –
      Sing out, children, as the little thrushes do –
Pluck you handfuls of the meadow-cowslips pretty –
      Laugh aloud, to feel your fingers let them through!
But they answer, 'Are your cowslips of the meadows
      Like our weeds anear the mine?
Leave us quiet in the dark of the coal-shadows,
      From your pleasures fair and fine!

'For oh,' say the children, 'we are weary,
      And we cannot run or leap –
If we cared for any meadows, it were merely
      To drop down in them and sleep.
Our knees tremble sorely in the stooping –
      We fall upon our faces, trying to go;
And, underneath our heavy eyelids drooping,
      The reddest flower would look as pale as snow.
For, all day, we drag our burden tiring,
      Through the coal-dark, underground –
Or, all day, we drive the wheels of iron
      In the factories, round and round.

'For, all day, the wheels are droning, turning, –
      Their wind comes in our faces, –
Till our hearts turn, – our heads, with pulses burning,
      And the walls turn in their places –
Turns the sky in the high window blank and reeling –
      Turns the long light that droppeth down the wall –
Turn the black flies that crawl along the ceiling –
      All are turning, all the day, and we with all! –
And all day, the iron wheels are droning;
      And sometimes we could pray,
"O ye wheels" (breaking out in a mad moaning),
      "Stop! be silent for to-day!"'

Ay! be silent! Let them hear each other breathing
  For a moment, mouth to mouth –
Let them touch each other's hands, in a fresh wreathing
  Of their tender human youth!
Let them feel that this cold metallic motion
  Is not all the life God fashions or reveals –
Let them prove their inward souls against the notion
  That they live in you, or under you, O wheels! –
Still, all day, the iron wheels go onward,
  As if Fate in each were stark;
And the children's souls, which God is calling sunward,
  Spin on blindly in the dark.

. . . .

'Two words, indeed, of praying we remember;
  And at midnight's hour of harm, –
"Our Father," looking upward in the chamber,
  We say softly for a charm.
We know no other words, except "Our Father,"
  And we think that, in some pause of angels' song,
God may pluck them with the silence sweet to gather,
  And hold both within His right hand which is strong.
"Our father!" If He heard us, He would surely
  (For they call Him good and mild)
Answer, smiling down the steep world very purely,
  "Come rest with me, my child."'
'But, no!' say the children, weeping faster,
  'He is speechless as a stone;'

. . . .

They look up with their pale and sunken faces,
    And their look is dread to see.
For they mind you of their angels in high places,
    With eyes turned on Deity.
'How long,' they say, 'how long, O cruel nation,
    Will you stand, to move the world on a child's heart, –
Stifle down with a mailed heel its palpitation,
    And tread onward to your throne amid the mart!
Our blood splashes upward, O gold-heaper,
    And your purple shows your path!
But the child's sob in the silence curses deeper
    Than the strong man in his wrath.'

ELIZABETH BARRETT BROWNING

ON SEEING AN OFFICER'S WIDOW DISTRACTED, WHO HAD BEEN DRIVEN TO DESPAIR BY A LONG AND FRUITLESS SOLICITATION FOR THE ARREARS OF HER PENSION

O wretch! hath madness cured thy dire despair?
Yes – All thy sorrows now are light as air:
No more you mourn your once loved husband's fate,
Who bravely perished for a thankless state.
For rolling years thy piety prevailed;
At length, quite sunk – thy hope, thy patience failed.
Distracted now you tread on life's last stage,
Nor feel the weight of poverty and age:
How blest in this, compared with those whose lot
Dooms them to miseries, by you forgot!

Now, wild as winds, you from your offspring fly,
Or fright them from you with distracted eye;
Rove through the streets; or sing, devoid of care,
With tattered garments and dishevelled hair;
By hooting boys to higher frenzy fired,
At length you sink, by cruel treatment tried,
Sink into sleep, an emblem of the dead,
A stone thy pillow, the cold earth thy bed.

O tell it not; let none the story hear,
Lest Britain's martial sons should learn to fear:
And when they next the hostile wall attack,
Feel the heart fail, the lifted arm grow slack;
And pausing cry – 'Though death we scorn to dread,
Our orphan offspring, must they pine for bread?
See their loved mothers into prisons thrown,
And, unrelieved, in iron bondage groan?'

Britain, for this impending ruin dread;
Their woes call loud for vengeance on thy head:
Nor wonder, if disasters wait your fleets;
Nor wonder at complainings in your streets.
Be timely wise; arrest th' uplifted hand,
Ere pestilence or famine sweep the land.

MARY BARBER

KITCHENETTE BUILDING

We are things of dry hours and the involuntary plan,
Grayed in, and gray. 'Dream' makes a giddy sound, not strong
Like 'rent', 'feeding a wife', 'satisfying a man'.

But could a dream send up through onion fumes
Its white and violet, fight with fried potatoes
And yesterday's garbage ripening in the hall,
Flutter, or sing an aria down these rooms.

Even if we were willing to let it in,
Had time to warm it, keep it very clean,
Anticipate a message, let it begin?

We wonder. But not well! not for a minute!
Since Number Five is out of the bathroom now,
We think of lukewarm water, hope to get in it.

GWENDOLYN BROOKS

THE CHOOSING

We were first equal Mary and I
with same coloured ribbons in mouse-coloured hair
and with equal shyness,
we curtseyed to the lady councillor
for copies of Collins' Children's Classics.
First equal, equally proud.

Best friends too Mary and I
a common bond in being cleverest (equal)
in our small school's small class.
I remember
the competition for top desk
or to read aloud the lesson
at school service.
And my terrible fear
of her superiority at sums.

I remember the housing scheme
where we both stayed.
The same houses, different homes,
where the choices were made.

I don't know exactly why they moved,
but anyway they went.
Something about a three-apartment
and a cheaper rent.
But from the top deck of the high-school bus
I'd glimpse among the others on the corner
Mary's father, mufflered, contrasting strangely
with the elegant greyhounds by his side.
He didn't believe in high school education,
especially for girls,
or in forking out for uniforms.

Ten years later on a Saturday –
I am coming from the library –
sitting near me on the bus,
Mary
with a husband who is tall,
curly haired, has eyes
for no one else but Mary.
Her arms are round the full-shaped vase
that is her body.
Oh, you can see where the attraction lies
in Mary's life –
not that I envy her, really.

And I am coming from the library
with my arms full of books.
I think of those prizes that were ours for the taking
and wonder when the choices got made
we don't remember making.

LIZ LOCHHEAD

A FATHER OF WOMEN

AD SOROREM E. B.

'Thy father was transfused into thy blood.'
Dryden, *Ode to Mrs Anne Killigrew*

Our father works in us,
The daughters of his manhood. Not undone
Is he, not wasted, though transmuted thus,
 And though he left no son.

Therefore on him I cry
To arm me: 'For my delicate mind a casque,
A breastplate for my heart, courage to die,
 Of thee, captain, I ask.

'Nor strengthen only; press
A finger on this violent blood and pale,
Over this rash will let thy tenderness
 A while pause, and prevail.

'And shepherd-father, thou
Whose staff folded my thoughts before my birth,
Control them now I am of earth, and now
 Thou art no more of earth.

'O liberal, constant, dear,
Crush in my nature the ungenerous art
Of the inferior; set me high, and here,
 Here garner up thy heart!'

Like to him now are they,
The million living fathers of the War –
Mourning the crippled world, the bitter day –
 Whose striplings are no more.

The crippled world! Come then,
Fathers of women with your honour in trust,
Approve, accept, know them daughters of men,
 Now that your sons are dust.

        ALICE MEYNELL

THE WOMAN'S LABOUR, AN EPISTLE

Immortal Bard! thou fav'rite of the Nine!
Enriched by peers, advanced by Caroline![1]
Deign to look down on one that's poor and low,
Rememb'ring you yourself was lately so;
Accept these lines; Alas! what can you have
From her, who ever was, and's still a slave?
No learning ever was bestowed on me;
My life was always spent in drudgery;
And not alone; alas! with grief I find,
It is the portion of poor woman-kind.
Oft have I thought as on my bed I lay,
Eased from the tiresome labours of the day,
Our first extraction from a mass refined,
Could never be for slavery designed;
Till time and custom by degrees destroyed
That happy state our sex at first enjoyed.
When men had used their utmost care and toil,
Their recompence was but a female smile;
When they by arts or arms were rendered great,
They laid their trophies at a woman's feet;
They, in those days, unto our sex did bring
Their hearts, their all, a free-will offering;
And as from us their being they derive,
They back again should all due homage give.

Jove once descending from the clouds did drop
In showers of gold on lovely Danae's[2] lap;
The sweet-tongued poets, in those generous days,
Unto our shrine still offered up their lays:
But now, alas! that Golden Age is past,
We are the objects of your scorn at last.
And you, great Duck, upon whose happy brow
The Muses seem to fix their garland now,
In your late poem boldly did declare
Alcides' labours[3] can't with yours compare,
And of your annual task have much to say,
Of threshing, reaping, mowing corn and hay;

[1] Queen Caroline awarded Stephen Duck a pension.

[2] The mother of Perseus.

[3] The labours of Hercules.

Boasting your daily toil, and nightly dream,
But can't conclude your never-dying theme
And let our hapless sex in silence lie
Forgotten, and in dark oblivion die,
But on our abject state you throw your scorn,
And women wrong, your verses to adorn.
You of hay-making speak a word or two,
As if our sex but little work could do:
This makes the honest farmer smiling say,
He'll seek for women still to make his hay,
For if his back be turned the work they mind
As well as men, as far as he can find.

    For my own part, I many a summer's day
Have spent in throwing, turning, making hay;
But ne'er could see, what you have lately found,
Our wages paid for sitting on the ground.
'Tis true, that when our morning's work is done,
And all our grass exposed unto the sun,
While that his scorching beams do on it shine,
As well as you we have the time to dine:
I hope, that since we freely toil and sweat
To earn our bread, you'll give us time to eat;
That over, soon we must get up again,
And nimbly turn our hay upon the plain;
Nay, rake and row it in, the case is clear,
Or how should cocks in equal rows appear?
But if you'd have what you have wrote believed,
I find, that you to hear us talk are grieved:
In this, I hope you do not speak your mind,
For none but Turks, that ever I could find,
Have mutes to serve them, or did e'er deny
Their slaves at work, to chat it merrily.
Since you have liberty to speak your mind,
And are to talk, as well as we, inclined,
Why should you thus repine, because that we,
Like you, enjoy that pleasing liberty?
What! would you lord it quite, and take away
The only privilege our sex enjoy?

When ev'ning does approach, we homeward hie
And our domestic toils incessant ply:
Against your coming home prepare to get
Our work all done, our house in order set;
Bacon and dumpling in the pot we boil,
Our beds we make, our swine we feed the while;
Then wait at door to see you coming home,
And set the table out against you come.
Early next morning we on you attend,
Our children dress and feed, their clothes we mend;
And in the field our daily task renew,
Soon as the rising sun has dried the dew.

When harvest comes, into the field we go,
And help to reap the wheat as well as you;
Or else we go the ears of corn to glean,
No labour scorning, be it e'er so mean;
But in the work we freely bear a part,
And what we can, perform with all our heart.
To get a living we so willing are,
Our tender babes unto the field we bear,
And wrap them in our clothes to keep them warm,
While round about we gather in the corn;
And often unto them our course do bend,
To keep them safe, that nothing them offend;
Our children that are able bear a share
In gleaning corn, such is our frugal care.
When night comes on, unto our home we go,
Our corn we carry, and our infant too,
Weary indeed! but 'tis not worth our while
Once to complain, or rest at ev'ry stile;
We must make haste, for when we home are come,
We find again our work but just begun;
So many things for our attendance call,
Had we ten hands, we could employ them all.
Our children put to bed, with greatest care
We all things for your coming home prepare:
You sup, and go to bed without delay,
And rest yourselves till the ensuing day;
While we, alas! but little sleep can have,
Because our froward children cry and rave;

Yet, without fail, soon as day-light doth spring,
We in the field again our work begin,
And there, with all our strength, our toil renew,
Till Titan's golden rays have dried the dew;
Then home we go unto our children dear,
Dress, feed, and bring them to the field with care.

Were this your case, you justly might complain
That day or night you're not secure from pain;
Those mighty troubles which perplex your mind
(Thistles before, and females come behind)
Would vanish soon, and quickly disappear,
Were you, like us, encumbered thus with care.
What you would have of us we do not know:
We oft take up the corn that you do mow,
We cut the peas, and always ready are
In every work to take our proper share;
And from the time that harvest doth begin,
Until the corn be cut and carried in,
Our toil and labour's daily so extreme,
That we have hardly ever time to dream.

The harvest ended, respite none we find;
The hardest of our toil is still behind;
Hard labour we most cheerfully pursue,
And out, abroad, a-charing often go,
Of which I now will briefly tell in part,
What fully to describe is past my art;
So many hardships daily we go through,
I boldly say, the like you never knew.

When bright Orion glitters in the skies
In winter nights, then early we must rise;
The weather ne'er so bad, wind, rain, or snow,
Our work appointed, we must rise and go,
While you on easy beds may lie and sleep,
Till light does through your chamber windows peep.
When to the house we come where we should go,
How to get in, alas! we do not know:
The maid quite tired with work the day before,
O'ercome with sleep; we standing at the door

Oppressed with cold, and often call in vain,
E'er to our work we can admittance gain;
But when from wind and weather we get in,
Briskly with courage we our work begin.
Heaps of fine linen we before us view,
Whereon to lay our strength and patience too;
Cambrics and muslins which our ladies wear,
Laces and edgings, costly, fine, and rare,
Which must be washed with utmost skill and care,
With holland shirts, ruffles and fringes too,
Fashions which our fore-fathers never knew.
For several hours here we work and slave,
Before we can one glimpse of day-light have;
We labour hard before the morning's past,
Because we fear the time runs on too fast.

At length bright Sol illuminates the skies,
And summons drowsy mortals to arise;
Then comes our mistress without fail,
And in her hand, perhaps, a mug of ale
To cheer our hearts, and also to inform
Herself what work is done that very morn;
Lays her commands upon us, that we mind
Her linen well, nor leave the dirt behind;
Nor this alone, but also to take care
We don't her cambrics nor her ruffles tear;
And these most strictly does of us require,
To save her soap, and sparing be of fire,
Tells us her charge is great, nay furthermore,
Her clothes are fewer than the time before.
Now we drive on, resolved our strength to try,
And what we can we do most willingly;
Until with heat and work, 'tis often known,
Not only sweat, but blood runs trickling down
Our wrists and fingers; still our work demands
The constant action of our lab'ring hands.

Now night comes on, from whence you have relief,
But that, alas! does but increase our grief:
With heavy hearts we often view the sun,
Fearing he'll set before our work be done,

For either in the morning, or at night,
We piece the summer's day with candle-light.
Though we all day with care our work attend,
Such is our fate, we know not when 'twill end;
When evening's come, you homeward take your way,
We, till our work is done, are forced to stay;
And after all our toil and labour past,
Six-pence or eight-pence pays us off at last;
For all our pains, no prospect can we see
Attend us, but old age and poverty.

The washing is not all we have to do:
We often change for work as well as you.
Our mistress of her pewter doth complain,
And 'tis our part to make it clean again.
This work, though very hard and tiresome too,
Is not the worst we hapless females do:
When night comes on, and we quite weary are,
We scarce can count what falls unto our share;
Pots, kettles, sauce-pans, skillets, we may see,
Skimmers, and ladles, and such trumpery,
Brought in to make complete our slavery.
Though early in the morning 'tis begun,
'Tis often very late before we've done;
Alas! our labours never know no end,
On brass and iron we our strength must spend;
Our tender hands and fingers scratch and tear;
All this, and more, with patience we must bear.
Coloured with dirt and filth we now appear;
Your threshing sooty peas will not come near.
All the perfections woman once could boast,
Are quite obscured, and altogether lost.

Once more our mistress sends to let us know
She wants our help, because the beer runs low;
Then in much haste for brewing we prepare,
The vessels clean, and scald with greatest care;
Often at midnight from our bed we rise,
At other times, ev'n that will not suffice;
Our work at ev'ning oft we do begin,
And ere we've done, the night comes on again.

Water we pump, the copper we must fill,
Or tend the fire; for if we e'er stand still,
Like you, when threshing, we a watch must keep,
Our wort boils over, if we dare to sleep.

But to rehearse all labour is in vain,
Of which we very justly might complain:
For us, you see, but little rest is found;
Our toil increases as the year runs round.
While you to Sisyphus yourselves compare,
With Danaus' daughters we may claim a share:
For while he labours hard against the hill,
Bottomless tubs of water they must fill.

So the industrious bees do hourly strive
To bring their loads of honey to the hive;
Their sordid owners always reap the gains,
And poorly recompense their toil and pains.

MARY COLLIER

From INSEC' LESSON

Todder nite mi a watch one program,
Yuh did watch it to Miss Vie?
De one wid de whole heap o' ants an' bug,
Mi couldn' believe mi yeye

When mi see ow de ants dem lib
An hep out one anedda,
So much hundred tousan ants
Dey wuk an' pull togedda.

De mooma ants she big an fat
So she liddung lay egg all day.
De solja ants tan up guard de door,
Mek sure no enemy no come dem way.

De worka ants a de bessis one,
Dem always wuk togedda
Fi feed de queen, an store de eggs,
An wash dem likkle bredda.

Some go out fi gadda food
Fi feed dose in de nes'
Some a dig hole fi mek new room
An some clean up de mess.

I' please mi fi see ow de ants dem pull,
An try fi get tings done,
Dem wuk an eat an sleep togedda
An a not even dem one.

Far mi see whole heap o' odda insect
Wasp, bug an fly an bee,
All a wuk togedda,
Ina perfec' harmony.

VALERIE BLOOM

THE TWO BOYS

I saw a boy with eager eye
Open a book upon a stall,
And read as he'd devour it all:
Which when the stall-man did espy,
Soon to the boy I heard him call,
'You, Sir, you never buy a book,
Therefore in one you shall not look.'
The boy passed slowly on, and with a sigh
He wish'd he never had been taught to read,
Then of the old churl's books he should have had no need.

   Of sufferings the poor have many,
Which never can the rich annoy.
I soon perceiv'd another boy
Who look'd as if he'd not had any
Food for that day at least, enjoy
The sight of cold meat in a tavern larder.
This boy's case, thought I, is surely harder,
Thus hungry longing, thus without a penny,
Beholding choice of dainty dressed meat:
No wonder if he wish he ne'er had learn'd to eat.

MARY LAMB

From A ROYAL PRINCESS

I a princess, king-descended, decked with jewels, gilded, drest,
Would rather be a peasant with her baby at her breast,
For all I shine so like the sun, and am purple like the west.

Two and two my guards behind, two and two before,
Two and two on either hand, they guard me evermore;
Me, poor dove that must not coo – eagle that must not soar.

All my fountains cast up perfumes, all my gardens grow
Scented woods and foreign spices, with all flowers in blow
That are costly, out of season as the seasons go.

All my walls are lost in mirrors, whereupon I trace
Self to right hand, self to left hand, self in every place,
Self-same solitary figure, self-same seeking face.

Then I have an ivory chair high to sit upon,
Almost like my father's chair, which is an ivory throne;
There I sit uplift and upright, there I sit alone.

Alone by day, alone by night, alone days without end;
My father and my mother give me treasures, search and spend –
O my father! O my mother! have you ne'er a friend?

As I am a lofty princess, so my father is
A lofty king, accomplished in all kingly subtilties,
Holding in his strong right hand world-kingdoms' balances.

.   .   .   .

My father counting up his strength sets down with equal pen
So many head of cattle, head of horses, head of men;
These for slaughter, these for labour, with the how and when.

Some to work on roads, canals; some to man his ships;
Some to smart in mines beneath sharp overseers' whips;
Some to trap fur-beasts in lands where utmost winter nips.

Once it came into my heart, and whelmed me like a flood,
That these too are men and women, human flesh and blood;
Men with hearts and men with souls, though trodden down like mud.

Our feasting was not glad that night, our music was not gay;
On my mother's graceful head I marked a thread of grey,
My father frowning at the fare seemed every dish to weigh.

I sat beside them sole princess in my exalted place,
My ladies and my gentlemen stood by me on the dais;
A mirror showed me I look old and haggard in the face;

It showed me that my ladies all are fair to gaze upon,
Plump, plenteous haired, to every one love's secret lore is known,
They laugh by day, they sleep by night; ah me, what is a throne?

. . . .

A day went by, a week went by. One day I heard it said:
'Men are clamouring, women, children, clamouring to be fed;
Men like famished dogs are howling in the streets for bread.'

So two whispered by my door, not thinking I could hear,
Vulgar naked truth, ungarnished for a royal ear;
Fit for cooping in the background, not to stalk so near.

But I strained my utmost sense to catch this truth, and mark:
'There are families out grazing, like cattle in the park.'
'A pair of peasants must be saved, even if we build an ark.'

A merry jest, a merry laugh, each strolled upon his way;
One was my page, a lad I reared and bore with day by day;
One was my youngest maid, as sweet and white as cream in May.

Other footsteps followed softly with a weightier tramp;
Voices said: 'Picked soldiers have been summoned from the camp,
To quell these base-born ruffians who make free to howl and stamp.'

'Howl and stamp?' one answered: 'They made free to hurl a stone
At the minister's state coach, well aimed and stoutly thrown.'
'There's work then for the soldiers, for this rank crop must be mown.'

'One I saw, a poor old fool with ashes on his head,
Whimpering because a girl had snatched his crust of bread:
Then he dropped; when some one raised him, it turned out he was
    dead.'

'After us the deluge,' was retorted with a laugh:
'If bread's the staff of life they must walk without a staff.'
'While I've a loaf they're welcome to my blessing and the chaff.'

These passed. 'The king:' stand up. Said my father with a smile:
'Daughter mine, your mother comes to sit with you awhile,
She's sad to-day, and who but you her sadness can beguile?'

He too left me. Shall I touch my harp now while I wait, –
(I hear them doubling guard below before our palace gate) –
Or shall I work the last gold stitch into my veil of state;

Or shall my woman stand and read some unimpassioned scene,
There's music of a lulling sort in words that pause between;
Or shall she merely fan me while I wait here for the queen?

Again I caught my father's voice in sharp word of command:
'Charge' a clash of steel: 'Charge again, the rebels stand.
Smite and spare not, hand to hand; smite and spare not, hand to
     hand.'

There swelled a tumult at the gate, high voices waxing higher;
A flash of red reflected light lit the cathedral spire;
I heard a cry for faggots, then I heard a yell for fire.

'Sit and roast there with your meat, sit and bake there with your bread,
You who sat to see us starve,' one shrieking woman said:
'Sit on your throne and roast with your crown upon your head.'

Nay, this thing will I do, while my mother tarrieth,
I will take my fine spun gold, but not to sew therewith,
I will take my gold and gems, and rainbow fan and wreath;

With a ransom in my lap, a king's ransom in my hand,
I will go down to this people, will stand face to face, will stand
Where they curse king, queen, and princess of this cursed land.

They shall take all to buy them bread, take all I have to give;
I, if I perish, perish; they to-day shall eat and live;
I, if I perish, perish; that's the goal I half conceive:

Once to speak before the world, rend bare my heart and show
The lesson I have learned, which is death, is life, to know.
I, if I perish, perish; in the name of God I go.

CHRISTINA ROSSETTI

WHEN THE NIGHT AND MORNING MEET

In the dark and narrow street,
  Into a world of woe,
Where the tread of many feet
  Went trampling to and fro,
A child was born – speak low!
When the night and morning meet.

Full seventy summers back
  Was this, so long ago,
The feet that wore the track
  Are lying straight and low;
Yet hath there been no lack
Of passers to and fro

Within the narrow street
  This childhood ever played;
Beyond the narrow street
  This manhood never strayed;
This age sat still and prayed
Anear the trampling feet.

The tread of ceaseless feet
  Flowed through his life, unstirred
By waters' fall, or fleet
  Wind music, or the bird
Of morn; these sounds are sweet,
But they were still unheard.

Within the narrow street
  I stood beside a bed,
  I held a dying head
When the night and morning meet;
And every word was sweet,
  Though few the words we said.

And as we talked, dawn drew
  To day, the world was fair
In fields afar, I knew;
  Yet spoke not to him there
Of how the grasses grew,
  Besprent with dewdrops rare.

We spoke not of the sun,
　　Nor of this green earth fair;
This soul, whose day was done,
　　Had never claimed its share
　　In these, and yet its rare
Rich heritage had won.

From the dark and narrow street.
　　Into a world of love
A child was born, – speak low,
Speak reverent, for we know
　　Not how they speak above,
When the night and morning meet.

DORA GREENWELL

From A MINOR PROPHET

I have a friend, a vegetarian seer,
By name Elias Baptist Butterworth,
A harmless, bland, disinterested man,
Whose ancestors in Cromwell's day believed
The Second Advent certain in five years,
But when King Charles the Second came instead,
Revised their date and sought another world:
I mean – not heaven but – America.
A fervid stock, whose generous hope embraced
The fortunes of mankind, not stopping short
At rise of leather, or the fall of gold,
Nor listening to the voices of the time
As housewives listen to a cackling hen,
With wonder whether she has laid her egg
On their own nest-egg. Still they did insist
Somewhat too wearisomely on the joys
Of their Millennium, when coats and hats
Would all be of one pattern, books and songs
All fit for Sundays, and the casual talk
As good as sermons preached extempore.

And in Elias the ancestral zeal
Breathes strong as ever, only modified
By Transatlantic air and modern thought.

. . . .

On all points he adopts the latest views;
Takes for the key of universal Mind
The 'levitation' of stout gentlemen;
Believes the Rappings are not spirits' work,
But the Thought-atmosphere's, a steam of brains
In correlated force of raps, as proved
By motion, heat, and science generally;
The spectrum, for example, which has shown
The self-same metals in the sun as here;
So the Thought-atmosphere is everywhere:
High truths that glimmered under other names
To ancient sages, whence good scholarship
Applied to Eleusinian mysteries –
The Vedas – Tripitaka – Vendidad –
Might furnish weaker proof for weaker minds
That Thought was rapping in the hoary past,
And might have edified the Greeks by raps
At the greater Dionysia, if their ears
Had not been filled with Sophoclean verse.
And when all Earth is vegetarian –
When, lacking butchers, quadrupeds die out,
And less Thought-atmosphere is reabsorbed
By nerves of insects parasitical,
Those higher truths, seized now by higher minds
But not expressed (the insects hindering)
Will either flash out into eloquence,
Or better still, be comprehensible
By rappings simply, without need of roots.

'Tis on this theme – the vegetarian world –
That good Elias willingly expands:
He loves to tell in mildly nasal tones
And vowels stretched to suit the widest views,
The future fortunes of our infant Earth –
When it will be too full of human kind
To have the room for wilder animals.
Saith he, Sahara will be populous
With families of gentlemen retired
From commerce in more Central Africa,
Who order coolness as we order coal,
And have a lobe anterior strong enough

To think away the sand-storms. Science thus
Will leave no spot on this terraqueous globe
Unfit to be inhabited by man,
The chief of animals: all meaner brutes
Will have been smoked and elbowed out of life.
No lions then shall lap Caffrarian pools,
Or shake the Atlas with their midnight roar:
Even the slow, slime-loving crocodile,
The last of animals to take a hint,
Will then retire for ever from a scene
Where public feeling strongly sets against him.
Fishes may lead carnivorous lives obscure,
But must not dream of culinary rank
Or being dished in good society.
Imagination in that distant age,
Aiming at fiction called historical,
Will vainly try to reconstruct the times
When it was men's preposterous delight
To sit astride live horses, which consumed
Materials for incalculable cakes;

. . . .

Boys will be boys, but dogs will all be moral,
With longer alimentary canals
Suited to diet vegetarian.
The uglier breeds will fade from memory,
Or, being palæontological,
Live but as portraits in large learned books,
Distasteful to the feelings of an age
Nourished on purest beauty. Earth will hold
No stupid brutes, no cheerful queernesses,
No naïve cunning, grave absurdity.
Wart-pigs with tender and parental grunts,
Wombats much flattened as to their contour,
Perhaps from too much crushing in the ark,
But taking meekly that fatality;
The serious cranes, unstung by ridicule;
Long-headed, short-legged, solemn-looking curs,
(Wise, silent critics of a flippant age);

The silly straddling foals, the weak-brained geese
Hissing fallaciously at sound of wheels –
All these rude products will have disappeared
Along with every faulty human type.
By dint of diet vegetarian
All will be harmony of hue and line,
Bodies and minds all perfect, limbs well-turned,
And talk quite free from aught erroneous.
Thus far Elias in his seer's mantle:
But at this climax in his prophecy
My sinking spirits, fearing to be swamped,
Urge me to speak. 'High prospects these, my friend,
Setting the weak carnivorous brain astretch;
We will resume the thread another day.'
'To-morrow,' cries Elias, 'at this hour?'
'No, not to-morrow – I shall have a cold –
At least I feel some soreness – this endemic –
Good-bye.'
         No tears are sadder than the smile
With which I quit Elias. Bitterly
I feel that every change upon this earth
Is bought with sacrifice. My yearnings fail
To reach that high apocalyptic mount
Which shows in bird's-eye view a perfect world,
Or enter warmly into other joys
Than those of faulty, struggling human kind.
That strain upon my soul's too feeble wing
Ends in ignoble floundering: I fall
Into short-sighted pity for the men
Who living in those perfect future times
Will not know half the dear imperfect things
That move my smiles and tears – will never know
The fine old incongruities that raise
My friendly laugh; the innocent conceits
That like a needless eyeglass or black patch
Give those who wear them harmless happiness;
The twists and cracks in our poor earthenware,
That touch me to more conscious fellowship
(I am not myself the finest Parian)
With my coevals.

. . . .

>   I cleave
> To nature's blunders, evanescent types
> Which sages banish from Utopia.
> 'Not worship beauty?' say you. Patience, friend!
> I worship in the temple with the rest;
> But by my hearth I keep a sacred nook
> For gnomes and dwarfs, duck-footed waddling elves
> Who stitched and hammered for the weary man
> In days of old. And in that piety
> I clothe ungainly forms inherited
> From toiling generations, daily bent
> At desk, or plough, or loom, or in the mine,
> In pioneering labours for the world.
> Nay, I am apt when floundering confused
> From too rash flight, to grasp at paradox,
> And pity future men who will not know
> A keen experience with pity blent,
> The pathos exquisite of lovely minds
> Hid in harsh forms –

GEORGE ELIOT

THE HUNTING OF THE HARE

Betwixt two *Ridges* of *Plowd-land*, lay *Wat*,
Pressing his *Body* close to *Earth* lay squat.
His *Nose* upon his two *Fore-feet* close lies,
Glaring obliquely with his *great gray Eyes*.
His *Head* he alwaies sets against the *Wind*;
If turne his *Taile*, his *Haires* blow up behind:
Which *he* too cold will grow, but *he* is wise,
And keepes his *Coat* still downe, so warm *he* lies.
Thus resting all the *day*, till *Sun* doth set,
Then riseth up, his *Reliefe* for to get.
Walking about untill the *Sun* doth rise,
Then back returnes, downe in his *Forme he* lyes.
At last, *Poore Wat* was found, as *he* there lay,
By *Hunts-men*, with their *Dogs* which came that way.
Seeing, gets up, and fast begins to run,
Hoping some waies the *Cruell Dogs* to shun.
But they by *Nature* have so quick a *Sent*,
That by their *Nose* they trace what way *he* went.

And with their deep, wide *Mouths* set forth a *Cry*,
Which answer'd was by *Ecchoes* in the *Skie*.
Then *Wat* was struck with *Terrour*, and with *Feare*,
Thinkes every *Shadow* still the *Dogs* they were.
And running out some distance from the *noise*,
To hide himselfe, his *Thoughts* he new imploies.
Under a *Clod* of *Earth* in *Sand-pit* wide,
Poore *Wat* sat close, hoping himselfe to hide.
There long he had not sat, but straight his *Eares*
The *Winding Hornes*, and crying *Dogs* he heares:
Starting with *Feare*, up leapes, then doth he run,
And with such speed, the *Ground* scarce treades upon.
Into a great thick *Wood he* strait way gets,
Where underneath a *broken Bough he* sits.
At every *Leafe* that with the *wind* did shake,
Did bring such *Terrour*, made his *Heart* to ake.
That *Place he* left, to *Champian Plaines he* went,
Winding about, to deceive their *Sent*.
And while they *snuffling* were, to find his *Track*,
Poore Wat, being weary, his swift pace did slack.
On his two *hinder legs* for ease did sit,
His *Fore-feet* rub'd his *Face* from *Dust*, and *Sweat*.
Licking his *Feet*, *he* wip'd his *Eares* so cleane,
That none could tell that *Wat* had hunted been.
But casting round about his *faire great Eyes*,
The *Hounds* in full *Careere* he neere him 'spies:
To *Wat* it was so terrible a *Sight*,
Feare gave him *Wings*, and made his *Body* light.
Though weary was before, by running long,
Yet now his *Breath* he never felt more strong.
Like those that *dying* are, think *Health* returnes,
When tis but a *faint Blast*, which *Life* out burnes.
For *Spirits* seek to guard the *Heart* about,
Striving with *Death*, but *Death* doth quench them out.
Thus they so fast came on, with such loud *Cries*,
That *he* no hopes hath left, nor *help* espies.
With that the *Winds* did pity *poore Wats* case,
And with their *Breath* the *Sent* blew from the *Place*.
Then every *Nose* is busily imployed,
And every *Nostrill* is set open, wide:
And every *Head* doth seek a severall way,

To find what *Grasse*, or *Track*, the *Sent* on lay.
Thus quick Industry, that is not slack,
Is like to Witchery, brings lost things back.
For though the *Wind* had tied the *Sent* up close,
A *Busie Dog* thrust in his *Snuffling Nose:*
And drew it out, with it did foremost run,
Then *Hornes* blew loud, for th' *rest* to follow on.
The *great slow-Hounds*, their throats did set a *Base*,
The *Fleet Swift Hounds*, as *Tenours* next in place;
The little *Beagles* they a *Trebble* sing,
And through the *Aire* their *Voice* a round did ring;
Which made a *Consort*, as they ran along;
If they but *words* could speak, might sing a *Song*,
The *Hornes* kept time, the *Hunters* shout for *Joy*,
And valiant seeme, *poore Wat* for to destroy:
Spurring their *Horses* to a full *Careere*,
Swim Rivers deep, leap Ditches without feare;
Indanger *Life*, and *Limbes*, so fast will ride,
Onely to see how patiently *Wat* died.
For why, the *Dogs* so neere his *Heeles* did get,
That they their sharp *Teeth* in his *Breech* did set.
Then tumbling downe, did fall with *weeping Eyes*,
Gives up his *Ghost*, and thus poore *Wat he* dies.
Men hooping loud, such *Acclamations* make,
As if the *Devill* they did *Prisoner* take.
When they do but a *shiftlesse Creature* kill;
To hunt, there needs no *Valiant Souldiers* skill.
But *Man* doth think that *Exercise*, and *Toile*,
To keep their *Health*, is best, which makes most spoile.
Thinking that *Food*, and *Nourishment* so good,
And *Appetite*, that feeds on *Flesh*, and *Blood*.
When they do *Lions, Wolves, Beares, Tigers* see,
To kill poore *Sheep*, strait say, they cruell be.
But for themselves all *Creatures* think too few,
For *Luxury*, wish *God* would make them new.
As if that *God* made *Creatures* for *Mans meat*,
To give them *Life*, and *Sense*, for *Man* to eat;
Or else for *Sport*, or *Recreations* sake,
Destroy those *Lifes* that *God* saw good to make:
Making their *Stomacks*, *Graves*, which full they fill
With *Murther'd Bodies*, that in sport they kill.

Yet *Man* doth think himselfe so gentle, mild,
When *he* of *Creatures* is most cruell wild.
And is so *Proud*, thinks only he shall live,
That *God* a *God*-like *Nature* did him give.
And that all *Creatures* for his sake alone,
Was made for him, to *Tyrannize* upon.

MARGARET CAVENDISH, DUCHESS OF NEWCASTLE

LUCKY

All things bright and beautiful
you loved your blameless cat
his name was LUCKY
lucky cat
fluffy and fat
a friend to all
and pure in thought word and deed

One night his luck ran out
chatted up, bundled off, sold
to men in white coats

Shaved from the neck to the end of his tail
Lucky was immersed
for twentyone days on end
in cold water
How long can he last
before going numb in his mind?

The other cats thought he was lucky
they were off their food
with the shocks

The puppy dog's head
on the old dog's neck
thought Lucky was lucky

The rats thought so
weeping blood

And so did the monkey
swinging in space
(later awarded the
V.D., T.B., and Order of Radiation)

And so did the newts
when their eyes were cut out
the better to see whether they needed them

And the cattle
in stocks
and the hens
in irons
every hope rolling away from them
they all thought Lucky was lucky

And he was
he died
God's last mercy

Watch it Lucky
even now
somebody
licensed to kill
by degrees
is working on
Eternal Life

GERDA MAYER

Literature and Art

THE poems in this section consider the importance of art, and especially of the poet's art, in other words, the creating of meaning through language and form. This is not easy, as you may have discovered yourself when doing your own writing. Why is it that what we want to say often eludes us? Is it because we can't quite find the right words and resort to stale clichés? And what can help restore to us the excitement of words? Elizabeth Jennings's 'A Performance of Henry V at Stratford-upon-Avon', Elinor Wylie's 'Bronze Trumpets and Sea Water' and U. A. Fanthorpe's 'Soothing and Awful' may suggest some answers to these questions. Does U. A. Fanthorpe imply it is the context or the nationality of the visitors which affects their verbal responses? Does her title involve a play on words? Would you say that irony is a feature of this poem? How does Elizabeth Jennings suggest that Shakespeare manages to 'renew our tongue'? Of an altogether richer and more allusive style is Elinor Wylie's 'Bronze Trumpets and Sea Water', which compares the very different qualities of English and Latin as languages. How effectively does her imagery convey those differences?

The element of craftsmanship is as important in writing as it is in other art and craft forms. The next two poems are about the mastery of those skills associated with particular crafts. Vita Sackville-West's 'All craftsmen share a knowledge' links poets with thatchers, pargetters and bricklayers. In what way does she suggest they are alike? Adrienne Rich's 'Aunt Jennifer's Tigers' features the visual craft of tapestry or embroidery. What makes it a consciously feminist poem? What does it have in common with Anne Finch's 'Melinda on an Insippid Beauty'? Christina Rossetti is less positive about the value of art than either Adrienne Rich or Anne Finch. For her, too, it can transcend or even subvert the material conditions of (a) human life, but that in itself is not necessarily a good thing. Her sonnet suggests the unreality or even falsity of art, particularly in its representations of women. 'In an Artist's Studio' is about her brother Dante Gabriel

Rossetti's Pre-Raphaelite paintings of Elizabeth Siddall. What do his paintings of her fail to recognize? Why do the last two lines of the poem repeat the same expression?

George Eliot's 'O, May I Join the Choir Invisible', which reads like a prayer for admittance to the circles of the great ones of the past, is about the nature of the literary ambition she entertained. What are the qualities of the great and the good that she aspires to emulate and be remembered for?

The early matriarchal world of feminist history features in the Malay legend of 'The White Women' as retold by Mary Elizabeth Coleridge. The poem also reveals the power of myth to subvert political and social notions of male dominance. Why does the poem begin with a question? What does the elemental imagery suggest in relation to these women? Would you say this is a hopeful or a despairing poem? Alice Walker is a contemporary black American poet and novelist who has rejected the term 'feminist' for 'womanist'. 'Songless' is about the power of art, whether it is the making of pots or poems. It might also be described as a political poem. How does Alice Walker link the two subjects and why? How does her poem compare in style and meaning with Emily Brontë's 'Silent is the House', which seems to be about the coming of poetic inspiration? Are their respective views of the imaginative process different or similar?

Finally, as Elizabeth Jennings's poem at the start of this section shows, poets often reflect on other poets' work as much as they do on life itself. The last three poems have been written with other poets firmly in mind. Wendy Cope's pastiche of W. S. Gilbert's 'A Policeman's Lot' is very clever because it takes the form and style of one poem and injects into it an understanding of the work of another and different poet (Ted Hughes). If you haven't already done so, listen to a recording of the Gilbert and Sullivan song and read some poetry by Ted Hughes. Is this pastiche (or imitation) a tribute or a send-up? How well does Cope imitate the Gilbertian style and capture Hughes's imaginative preoccupations?

Emily Dickinson's much more serious and exalted poem 'I think I was enchanted' pays tribute to the spell that another woman poet, 'that foreign lady', Elizabeth Barrett Browning, cast on her when she first encountered her poetry. How did this spell manifest itself? It clearly wrought a momentous change in her perception of life and in particular of the most insignificant of its creatures. Do you think this changed perception involves herself as woman and poet? 'The Season's Lovers' by the Canadian poet Miriam Waddington has clearly been inspired by the sixteenth-century English poet John Donne's 'The Sunne Rising' about his love for his wife, Ann. If you don't already know that poem, try to read it. How does Miriam Waddington extend our understanding of Donne's poem? Is it necessary to know of the source of 'The Season's Lovers' to appreciate or understand it?

'SOOTHING AND AWFUL'

(Visitors' Book at Montacute church)

You are meant to exclaim. The church
Expects it of you. Bedding plants
And polished brass anticipate a word.

Visitors jot a name
A nationality, briskly enough,
But find *Remarks* beyond them.

I love English churches!
Says Friedrichshafen expansively.
The English are more backward. They come,

Certainly, from Spalding, Westbury-on-Trym,
The Isle of Wight; but all the words
They know are: *Very Lovely; Very Peaceful; Nice.*

A giggling gaggle from Torquay Grammar,
All pretending they can't spell *beautiful*, concoct
A private joke about the invisible organ.

A civilized voice from Cambridge
Especially noticed the well-kept churchyard.
Someone from Dudley, whose writing suggests tight shoes,

Reported *Nice and Cool.* The young entry
Yelp their staccato approval:
Super! Fantastic! Jesus Lives! Ace!

But what they found,
Whatever it was, it wasn't what
They say. In the beginning,

We know, the word, but not here,
Land of the perpetually-flowering cliché,
The rigid lip. Our fathers who piled

Stone upon stone, our mothers
Who stitched the hassocks, our cousins
Whose bones lie smooth, harmonious around –

However majestic their gifts, comely their living,
Their words would be thin like ours; they would join
In our inarticulate anthem: *Very Cosy.*

U. A. FANTHORPE

A PERFORMANCE OF HENRY V
AT STRATFORD-UPON-AVON

Nature teaches us our tongue again
And the swift sentences come pat. I came
Into cool night rescued from rainy dawn.
And I seethed with language – Henry at
Harfleur and Agincourt came apt for war
In Ireland and the Middle East. Here was
The riddling and right tongue, the feeling words
Solid and dutiful. Aspiring hope
Met purpose in 'advantages' and 'He
That fights with me today shall be my brother.'
Say this is patriotic, out of date.
But you are wrong. It never is too late

For nights of stars and feet that move to an
Iambic measure; all who clapped were linked,
The theatre is our treasury and too,
Our study, school-room, house where mercy is

Dispensed with justice. Shakespeare has the mood
And draws the music from the dullest heart.
This is our birthright, speeches for the dumb
And unaccomplished. Henry has the words
For grief and we learn how to tell of death
With dignity. 'All was as cold' she said
'As any stone' and so, we who lacked scope
For big or little deaths, increase, grow up
To purposes and means to face events
Of cruelty, stupidity. I walked
Fast under stars. The Avon wandered on
'Tomorrow and tomorrow'. Words aren't worn
Out in this place but can renew our tongue,
Flesh out our feeling, make us apt for life.

ELIZABETH JENNINGS

BRONZE TRUMPETS AND SEA WATER –
ON TURNING LATIN INTO ENGLISH

Alembics turn to stranger things
Strange things, but never while we live
Shall magic turn this bronze that sings
To singing water in a sieve.

The trumpeters of Caesar's guard
Salute his rigorous bastions
With ordered bruit; the bronze is hard
Though there is silver in the bronze.

Our mutable tongue is like the sea,
Curled wave and shattering thunder-fit;
Dangle in strings of sand shall he
Who smooths the ripples out of it.

ELINOR WYLIE

From THE LAND

All craftsmen share a knowledge. They have held
Reality down fluttering to a bench;
Cut wood to their own purposes; compelled
The growth of pattern with the patient shuttle;
Drained acres to a trench.
Control is theirs. They have ignored the subtle
Release of spirit from the jail of shape.
They have been concerned with prison, not escape;
Pinioned the fact, and let the rest go free,
And out of need made inadvertent art.
All things designed to play a faithful part
Build up their plain particular poetry.
Tools have their own integrity;
The sneath of scythe curves rightly to the hand,
The hammer knows its balance, knife its edge,
All tools inevitably planned,
Stout friends, with pledge
Of service; with their crotchets too
That masters understand,
And proper character, and separate heart,
But always to their chosen temper true.

– So language, smithied at the common fire,
Grew to its use; as sneath and shank and haft
Of well-grained wood, nice instruments of craft,
Curve to the simple mould the hands require,
Born of the needs of man.
The poet like the artisan
Works lonely with his tools; picks up each one,
Blunt mallet knowing, and the quick thin blade,
And plane that travels when the hewing's done;
Rejects, and chooses; scores a fresh faint line;
Sharpens, intent upon his chisellings;
Bends lower to examine his design,
If it be truly made,
And brings perfection to so slight a thing.
But in the shadows of his working-place,
Dust-moted, dim,
Among the chips and lumber of his trade,
Lifts never his bowed head, a breathing-space
To look upon the world beyond the sill,
The world framed small, in distance, for to him
The world and all its weight are in his will.
Yet in the ecstasy of his rapt mood
There's no retreat his spirit cannot fill,
No distant leagues, no present, and no past,
No essence that his need may not distil,
All pressed into his service, but he knows
Only the immediate care, if that be good;
The little focus that his words enclose;
As the poor joiner, working at his wood,
Knew not the tree from which the planks were taken,
Knew not the glade from which the trunk was brought,
Knew not the soil in which the roots were fast,
Nor by what centuries of gales the boughs were shaken,
But holds them all beneath his hands at last.

Much goes to little making, – law and skill,
Tradition's usage, each man's separate gift;
Till the slow worker sees that he has wrought
More than he knew of builded truth,
As one who slips through years of youth,
Leaving his young indignant rage,
And finds the years' insensible drift
Brings him achievement with the truce of age.

VITA SACKVILLE-WEST

AUNT JENNIFER'S TIGERS

Aunt Jennifer's tigers prance across a screen,
Bright topaz denizens of a world of green.
They do not fear the men beneath the tree;
They pace in sleek chivalric certainty.

Aunt Jennifer's fingers fluttering through her wool
Find even the ivory needle hard to pull.
The massive weight of Uncle's wedding band
Sits heavily upon Aunt Jennifer's hand.

When Aunt is dead, her terrified hands will lie
Still ringed with ordeals she was mastered by.
The tigers in the panel that she made
Will go on prancing, proud and unafraid.

ADRIENNE RICH

MELINDA ON AN INSIPPID BEAUTY
In imitation of a fragment of Sappho's

You, when your body life shall leave
Must drop entire, into the grave;
Unheeded, unregarded lie,
And all of you together die;
Must hide that fleeting charm, that face in dust,
Or to some painted cloth, the slighted Image trust,
Whilst my fam'd works, shall through all times surprise
My polish'd thoughts, my bright Ideas rise,
And to new men be known, still talking to their eyes.

ANNE FINCH

IN AN ARTIST'S STUDIO

One face looks out from all his canvases,
 One selfsame figure sits or walks or leans:
 We found her hidden just behind those screens,
That mirror gave back all her loveliness.
A queen in opal or in ruby dress,
 A nameless girl in freshest summer-greens,
 A saint, an angel – every canvas means
The same one meaning, neither more nor less.
He feeds upon her face by day and night,
 And she with true kind eyes looks back on him,
Fair as the moon and joyful as the light:
 Not wan with waiting, nor with sorrow dim;
Not as she is, but was when hope shone bright;
 Not as she is, but as she fills his dream.

CHRISTINA ROSSETTI

'O MAY I JOIN THE CHOIR INVISIBLE'

Longum illud tempus, quum non ero, magis me movet, quam hoc exiguum.
Cicero, *ad Att.*, xii. 18

O may I join the choir invisible
Of those immortal dead who live again
In minds made better by their presence: live
In pulses stirred to generosity,
In deeds of daring rectitude, in scorn
For miserable aims that end with self,
In thoughts sublime that pierce the night like stars,
And with their mild persistence urge man's search
To vaster issues.
                     So to live in heaven:
To make undying music in the world,
Breathing as beauteous order that controls
With growing sway the growing life of man.
So we inherit that sweet purity
For which we struggled, failed, and agonised
With widening retrospect that bred despair.

Rebellious flesh that would not be subdued,
A vicious parent shaming still its child
Poor anxious penitence, is quick dissolved;
Its discords, quenched by meeting harmonies,
Die in the large and charitable air.
And all our rarer, better, truer self,
That sobbed religiously in yearning song,
That watched to ease the burthen of the world,
Laboriously tracing what must be,
And what may yet be better – saw within
A worthier image for the sanctuary,
And shaped it forth before the multitude
Divinely human, raising worship so
To higher reverence more mixed with love –
That better self shall live till human Time
Shall fold its eyelids, and the human sky
Be gathered like a scroll within the tomb
Unread for ever.
            This is life to come,
Which martyred men have made more glorious
For us who strive to follow. May I reach
That purest heaven, be to other souls
The cup of strength in some great agony,
Enkindle generous ardour, feed pure love,
Beget the smiles that have no cruelty –
Be the sweet presence of a good diffused,
And in diffusion ever more intense.
So shall I join the choir invisible
Whose music is the gladness of the world.

GEORGE ELIOT

THE WHITE WOMEN

('From a legend of Malay, told by Hugh Clifford')

Where dwell the lovely, wild white women folk,
    Mortal to man?
They never bowed their necks beneath the yoke,
They dwelt alone when the first morning broke
    And Time began.

Taller are they than man, and very fair,
    Their cheeks are pale,
At sight of them the tiger in his lair,
The falcon hanging in the azure air,
    The eagles quail.

The deadly shafts their nervous hands let fly
    Are stronger than our strongest – in their form
Larger, more beauteous, carved amazingly,
And when they fight, the wild white women cry
    The war-cry of the storm.

Their words are not as ours. If man might go
    Among the waves of Ocean when they break
And hear them – hear the language of the snow
Falling on torrents – he might also know
    The tongue they speak.

Pure are they as the light; they never sinned,
    But when the rays of the eternal fire
Kindle the West, their tresses they unbind
And fling their girdles to the Western wind,
    Swept by desire.

Lo, maidens to the maidens then are born,
    Strong children of the maidens and the breeze,
Dreams are not – in the glory of the morn,
Seen through the gates of ivory and horn –
    More fair than these.

And none may find their dwelling. In the shade
    Primeval of the forest oaks they hide.
One of our race, lost in an awful glade,
Saw with his human eyes a wild white maid,
    And gazing, died.
          MARY ELIZABETH COLERIDGE

SONGLESS

What is the point
of being artists
if we cannot save our life?
That is the cry
that wakes us
in our sleep.
Being happy is not the only
happiness.
And how many gadgets
can one person manage
at one time?

Over in the Other World
the women count
their wealth
in empty
calabashes.
How to transport
food
from watering hole
to watering
hole
has ceased to be
a problem
since the animals
died
and seed grain shrunk
to fit the pocket.

Now
it is just a matter
of who can create
the finest
decorations
on the empty
pots.

They say in Nicaragua
the whole
government
writes,
makes music
and paints,
saving their own
and helping the people save
their own lives.

(I ask you to notice
who, songless,
rules us
here.)

They say in Nicaragua
the whole
government
writes
and makes
music
saving its own
and helping the people save
their own lives.
These are not containers
void of food.
These are not decorations
on empty pots.

ALICE WALKER

SILENT IS THE HOUSE

Silent is the House – all are laid asleep;
One, alone, looks out o'er the snow-wreaths deep;
Watching every cloud, dreading every breeze
That whirls the 'wildering drifts and bends the groaning trees.

Cheerful is the hearth, soft the matted floor;
Not one shivering gust creeps through pane or door
The little lamp burns straight; its rays shoot strong and far;
I trim it well to be the Wanderer's guiding-star.

Frown, my haughty sire, chide my angry dame;
Set your slaves to spy, threaten me with shame;
But neither sire nor dame, nor prying serf shall know
What angel nightly tracks that waste of winter snow.

.   .   .   .

'He comes with western winds, with evening's wandering airs,
With that clear dusk of heaven that brings the thickest stars;
Winds take a pensive tone, and stars a tender fire,
And visions rise and change which kill me with desire

'Desire for nothing known in my maturer years
When joy grew mad with awe at counting future tears;
When, if my spirit's sky was full of flashes warm,
I knew not whence they came, from sun or thunderstorm;

'But first a hush of peace, a soundless calm descends;
The struggle of distress and fierce impatience ends;
Mute music soothes my breast – unuttered harmony
That I could never dream till earth was lost to me.

'Then dawns the Invisible, the Unseen its truth reveals;
My outward sense is gone, my inward essence feels –
Its wings are almost free, its home, its harbour found;
Measuring the gulf it stoops and dares the final bound!

'Oh, dreadful is the check – intense the agony
When the ear begins to hear and the eye begins to see;
When the pulse begins to throb, the brain to think again,
The soul to feel the flesh and the flesh to feel the chain!

'Yet I would lose no sting, would wish no torture less;
The more that anguish racks the earlier it will bless;
And robed in fires of Hell, or bright with heavenly shine,
If it but herald Death, the vision is divine.'

EMILY BRONTË

A POLICEMAN'S LOT

The progress of any writer is marked by those moments when he manages to outwit his own inner police system.

TED HUGHES

Oh, once I was a policeman young and merry (young and merry),
Controlling crowds and fighting petty crime (petty crime),
But now I work on matters literary (litererry)
And I am growing old before my time ('fore my time).
No, the imagination of a writer (of a writer)
Is not the sort of beat a chap would choose (chap would choose)
And they've assigned me a prolific blighter ('lific blighter) –
I'm patrolling the unconscious of Ted Hughes.

It's not the sort of beat a chap would choose (chap would choose) –
Patrolling the unconscious of Ted Hughes.

All our leave was cancelled in the lambing season (lambing season),
When bitter winter froze the drinking trough (drinking trough),
For our commander stated, with good reason (with good reason),
That that's the kind of thing that starts him off (starts him off).
But anything with four legs causes trouble (causes trouble) –
It's worse than organizing several zoos (several zoos),
Not to mention mythic creatures in the rubble (in the rubble),
Patrolling the unconscious of Ted Hughes.

It's worse than organizing several zoos (several zoos),
Patrolling the unconscious of Ted Hughes.

Although it's disagreeable and stressful (bull and stressful)
Attempting to avert poetic thought ('etic thought),
I could boast of times when I have been successful (been successful)
And conspiring compound epithets were caught ('thets were caught).
But the poetry statistics in this sector (in this sector)
Are enough to make a copper turn to booze (turn to booze)
And I do not think I'll make it to inspector (to inspector)
Patrolling the unconscious of Ted Hughes.

It's enough to make a copper turn to booze (turn to booze) –
Patrolling the unconscious of Ted Hughes.

WENDY COPE (AFTER W.S. GILBERT)

I THINK I WAS ENCHANTED

I think I was enchanted
When first a sombre girl,
I read that foreign lady,
The dark, felt beautiful.

And whether it was noon at night
Or only heaven at noon,
For very lunacy of light
I had not power to tell.

The bees became as butterflies,
The butterflies as swans
Approached and spurned the narrow grass
And just the meanest tunes

That nature murmured to herself
To keep herself in cheer,
I took for giants practising
Titanic opera.

The days to mighty metres stept.
The homeliest adorned
As if unto a jubilee
'Twere suddenly confirmed

I could not have defined the change.
Conversion of the mind
Like sanctifying in the soul
Is witnessed not explained.

'Twas a divine insanity.
The Danger to be Sane
Should I again experience,
'Tis antidote to turn

To tomes of solid witchcraft
Magicians be asleep
But magic hath an element
Like deity to keep.

EMILY DICKINSON

THE SEASON'S LOVERS

In the daisied lap of summer
The lovers lay, they dozed
And lay in sun unending,
They lay in light, they slept
And only stirred
Each one to find the other's lips.
At times they sighed
Or spoke a word
That wavered on uneven breath,
He had no name and she forgot
The ransomed kingdom of her death.

When at last the sun went down
And chilly evening stained the fields,
The lovers rose and rubbed their eyes:
They saw the pale wash of grass
Heighten to metallic green
And spindly tongues of granite mauve
Lick up the milk of afternoon,
They gathered all the scattered light
Of daisies to one place of white,
And ghostly poets lent their speech
To the stillness of the air,
The lovers listened, each to each.

Into the solid wall of night,
The lovers looked, their clearer sight
Went through that dark intensity
To the other side of light.
The lovers stood, it seemed to them
They hung upon the world's rim –
He clung to self, and she to him;
He rocked her with his body's hymn
And murmured to her shuddering cry,
You are all states, all princes I.
And sang against her trembling limbs,
Nothing else is, he sang, *but I.*

They lifted the transparent lid
From world false and world true
And in the space of both they flew.
He found a name, she lost her death,
And summer lulled them in its lap
With leafy lullaby.
There they sleep unending sleep,
The lovers lie
He with a name, she free of death,
In a country hard to find
Unless you read love's double mind
Or invent its polar map.

MIRIAM WADDINGTON

Separation and Suffering

THE poems in this section give voice to feelings of distress that stem from a sense of what our modern age has called 'alienation'. This sense of being cut off or estranged from one's own kind or even from one's own self is something that women as well as men have experienced and it dates back to Anglo-Saxon times at least, as 'Eadwacer' makes clear. Like 'The Wife's Lament', which it closely resembles, the poem regrets the separation that the woman is forced to endure, cut off from her own people and her beloved. Similarly, 'Patterns' and 'To Mrs M. A. upon Absence' are also about the pain of separation. How does Katherine Philips's and Amy Lowell's sense of loss at enforced absence or even death compare with Eadwacer's lament? Which is the most emotional of the three poems? Which is apparently the least emotional? How can you tell? What is the significance of Amy Lowell's title and how many different patterns does her poem suggest?

Distress and anguish are turned inwards in the following three poems, 'The Other Side of a Mirror', 'No Crooked Leg' and 'I am the only being'. What does Mary Elizabeth Coleridge regret in 'The Other Side of a Mirror'? How might her feelings be described as destructive? Does Queen Elizabeth I share her sense of self-hatred in 'No crooked leg'? Compare Elizabeth I's generalized comment on the withering effects of suspicion, something she must have known from her personal experience, with Emily Brontë's 'I am the only being'. Is Brontë lamenting limited opportunities and a wasted life? Which of these three poems do you find the most despairing and why?

In 'Lineage' Margaret Walker, a black American poet, suggests she has lost touch with her roots. How has this come about? What aspects does she regret losing? George Eliot's final sonnet in her sequence of eleven about her childhood love for her brother is shot through with the anguish of their later estrangement. How well does George Eliot employ the Shakespearean form of the sonnet? Look at the division of lines into 8, 4, and 2. Do you find it a positive or overwhelmingly sad poem?

The next two poems are about the isolation that sadness imposes. Ella Wheeler Wilcox's 'Solitude' was an extremely popular poem in the late nineteenth century and early twentieth century, and was frequently anthologized. Can you suggest why this was so? Christina Rossetti's sense of intense pain in 'A Better Resurrection' resembles Mary Elizabeth Coleridge's in 'The Other Side of a Mirror'. Is her situation as clear as Coleridge's? Look closely at her imagery. Does it matter that it is not striking or original?

Sylvia Plath's 'Paralytic' is also about the isolation that pain imposes on individuals. It describes her father in an oxygen tent after a serious collapse. How does her poem's sense of suffering differ from Rossetti's? Despite its title, 'Address to My Soul' is a much less personal poem in that it looks at the isolation of the individual self – or soul – in a general sense. Does the poem accept this separation without fear or distress? How would you describe the tone of this poem – impersonal, rational, unemotional? Would you say that it is a religious poem? Is the simplicity of the poem's form matched by its diction and imagery?

Dorothy Wordsworth's 'Floating Island at Hawkshead' depicts a strangely resonant incident she observed on one of her regular walks around her home in the Lake District. How does this poem compare with Elinor Wylie's in its attitude to separation? Is it reluctant, resigned, guardedly positive, optimistic? Why does it remind us of John Donne's 'No Man Is an Island'? In what way can her own situation as unrecognized inspirer of her more famous brother be read into this poem, despite its studiedly impersonal appearance?

EADWACER

It is to my own as if the man made them a gift:
If trouble comes on him, they will take him in;
With us it is otherwise.

Wulf is on an island, I on another.
It is a fastness, that island, the fens ring it.

Lusty fighters live on the island:
If trouble comes on him, they will take him in;
With us it is otherwise.

I waited for my wanderer, my Wulf, hoping and fearing:
When it was rainy weather and I sat wretched, weeping;
When the doughty man drew me into his arms –
It was heaven, yes, but hateful, too.

Wulf, my Wulf, waiting for thee
Hath left me sick, so seldom hast thou come;
A starving mood, no stint of meat.

Hearest thou, Eadwacer? Our whelp is borne off,
A wolf bears him to the woods.

It takes little to loose a link never made,
Our gladness together.

Translated by KEMP MALONE

TO MRS M.A. UPON ABSENCE

'Tis now since I began to die
    Four months, yet still I gasping live;
Wrapp'd up in sorrow do I lie,
    Hoping, yet doubting a reprieve.
Adam from Paradise expell'd
Just such a wretched being held.

'Tis not thy love I fear to lose,
    That will in spite of absence hold;
But 'tis the benefit and use
    Is lost, as in imprison'd gold:
Which though the sum be ne'er so great,
Enriches nothing but conceit.

What angry star then governs me
    That I must feel a double smart,
Prisoner to fate as well as thee;
    Kept from thy face, link'd to thy heart?
Because my love all love excels,
Must my grief have no parallels?

Sapless and dead as Winter here
    I now remain, and all I see
Copies of my wild state appear,
    But I am their epitome.
Love me no more, for I am grown
Too dead and dull for thee to own.

KATHERINE PHILIPS

PATTERNS

I walk down the garden paths,
And all the daffodils
Are blowing, and the bright blue squills.
I walk down the patterned garden-paths
In my stiff, brocaded gown.
With my powdered hair and jewelled fan,
I too am a rare
Pattern. As I wander down
The garden paths.

My dress is richly figured,
And the train
Makes a pink and silver stain
On the gravel, and the thrift
Of the borders.
Just a plate of current fashion,
Tripping by in high-heeled, ribboned shoes.
Not a softness anywhere about me,
Only whalebone and brocade.
And I sink on a seat in the shade
Of a lime tree. For my passion
Wars against the stiff brocade.
The daffodils and squills
Flutter in the breeze
As they please.
And I weep;
For the lime-tree is in blossom
And one small flower has dropped upon my bosom.

And the plashing of waterdrops
In the marble fountain
Comes down the garden-paths.
The dripping never stops.
Underneath my stiffened gown
Is the softness of a woman bathing in a marble basin,
A basin in the midst of hedges grown
So thick, she cannot see her lover hiding,
But she guesses he is near,
And the sliding of the water
Seems the stroking of a dear
Hand upon her.

What is Summer in a fine brocaded gown!
I should like to see it lying in a heap upon the ground.
All the pink and silver crumpled up on the ground.

I would be the pink and silver as I ran along the paths,
And he would stumble after,
Bewildered by my laughter.
I should see the sun flashing from his sword-hilt and the buckles on
    his shoes.
I would choose
To lead him in a maze along the patterned paths,
A bright and laughing maze for my heavy-booted lover.
Till he caught me in the shade,
And the buttons of his waistcoat bruised my body as he clasped me,
Aching, melting, unafraid.
With the shadows of the leaves and the sundrops,
And the plopping of the waterdrops,
All about us in the open afternoon –
I am very like to swoon
With the weight of this brocade,
For the sun sifts through the shade.

Underneath the fallen blossom
In my bosom,
Is a letter I have hid.
It was brought to me this morning by a rider from the Duke.
'Madam, we regret to inform you that Lord Hartwell
Died in action Thursday se'nnight.'
As I read it in the white, morning sunlight,
The letters squirmed like snakes.
'Any answer, Madam,' said my footman.
'No,' I told him.
'See that the messenger takes some refreshment.
No, no answer.'
And I walked into the garden,
Up and down the patterned paths,
In my stiff, correct brocade.
The blue and yellow flowers stood up proudly in the sun,
Each one.

I stood upright too,
Held rigid to the pattern
By the stiffness of my gown.
Up and down I walked,
Up and down.

In a month he would have been my husband.
In a month, here, underneath this lime,
We would have broke the pattern;
He for me, and I for him,
He as Colonel, I as Lady,
On this shady seat.
He had a whim
That sunlight carried blessing.
And I answered, 'It shall be as you have said.'
Now he is dead.

In Summer and in Winter I shall walk
Up and down
The patterned garden-paths
In my stiff, brocaded gown.
The squills and daffodils
Will give place to pillared roses, and to asters, and to snow.
I shall go
Up and down,
In my gown.
Gorgeously arrayed,
Boned and stayed.
And the softness of my body will be guarded from embrace
By each button, hook and lace.
For the man who should loose me is dead,
Fighting with the Duke in Flanders,
In a pattern called a war.
Christ! What are patterns for?

AMY LOWELL

THE OTHER SIDE OF A MIRROR

I sat before my glass one day,
　　And conjured up a vision bare,
Unlike the aspects glad and gay,
　　That erst were found reflected there –
The vision of a woman, wild
　　With more than womanly despair.

Her hair stood back on either side
　　A face bereft of loveliness.
It had no envy now to hide
　　What once no man on earth could guess.
It formed the thorny aureole
　　Of hard unsanctified distress.

Her lips were open – not a sound
　　Came through the parted lines of red.
Whate'er it was, the hideous wound
　　In silence and in secret bled.
No sigh relieved her speechless woe,
　　She had no voice to speak her dread.

And in her lurid eyes there shone
　　The dying flame of life's desire,
Made mad because its hope was gone,
　　And kindled at the leaping fire
Of jealousy, and fierce revenge,
　　And strength that could not change nor tire.

Shade of a shadow in the glass,
　　O set the crystal surface free!
Pass – as the fairer visions pass –
　　Nor ever more return, to be
The ghost of a distracted hour,
　　That heard me whisper, 'I am she!'

　　　　　MARY ELIZABETH COLERIDGE

WRITTEN IN HER FRENCH PSALTER

No crooked leg, no bleared eye,
No part deformed out of kind,
Nor yet so ugly half can be
As is the inward suspicious mind.

ELIZABETH I

I AM THE ONLY BEING

I am the only being whose doom
No tongue would ask, no eye would mourn;
I never caused a thought of gloom,
A smile of joy, since I was born.

In secret pleasure, secret tears,
This changeful life has slipped away,
As friendless after eighteen years,
As lone as on my natal day.

There have been times I cannot hide,
There have been times when this was drear,
When my sad soul forgot its pride
And longed for one to love me here.

But those were in the early glow
Of feelings not subdued by care;
And they have died so long ago;
I hardly now believe they were.

First melted off the hope of youth,
Then Fancy's rainbow fast withdrew;
And they have died so long ago,
In mortal bosoms never grew.

'Twas grief enough to think mankind
All hollow, servile, insincere;
But worse to trust to my own mind
And find the same corruption there.

EMILY BRONTË

LINEAGE

My grandmothers were strong.
They followed plows and bent to toil.
They moved through fields sowing seed.
They touched earth and grain grew.
They were full of sturdiness and singing.
My grandmothers were strong.

My grandmothers are full of memories
Smelling of soap and onions and wet clay
With veins rolling roughly over quick hands
They have many clean words to say.
My grandmothers were strong.
Why am I not as they?

MARGARET WALKER

From BROTHER AND SISTER SONNETS

II

School parted us; we never found again
That childish world where our two spirits mingled
Like scents from varying roses that remain
One sweetness, nor can evermore be singled.

Yet the twin habit of that early time
Lingered for long about the heart and tongue;
We had been natives of one happy clime,
And its dear accent to our utterance clung.

Till the dire years whose awful name is Change
Had grasped our souls still yearning in divorce,
And pitiless shaped them in two forms that range
Two elements which sever their life's course.

But were another childhood-world my share,
I would be born a little sister there.

GEORGE ELIOT

SOLITUDE

Laugh, and the world laughs with you;
   Weep, and you weep alone,
For the sad old earth must borrow its mirth,
   But has trouble enough of its own.
Sing, and the hills will answer;
   Sigh, it is lost on the air,
The echoes bound to a joyful sound,
   But shrink from voicing care.

Rejoice, and men will seek you;
   Grieve, and they turn and go.
They want full measure of all your pleasure,
   But they do not need your woe.
Be glad, and your friends are many;
   Be sad, and you lose them all, –
There are none to decline your nectar'd wine,
   But alone you must drink life's gall.

Feast, and your halls are crowded;
   Fast, and the world goes by.
Succeed and give, and it helps you live,
   But no man can help you die.
There is room in the halls of pleasure
   For a large and lordly train,
But one by one we must all file on
   Through the narrow aisles of pain.

ELLA WHEELER WILCOX

A BETTER RESURRECTION

I have no wit, no words, no tears;
   My heart within me like a stone
Is numbed too much for hopes or fears.
   Look right, look left, I dwell alone;
I lift mine eyes, but dimmed with grief
   No everlasting hills I see;
My life is in the falling leaf:
   O Jesus, quicken me.

My life is like a faded leaf,
   My harvest dwindled to a husk:
Truly my life is void and brief
   And tedious in the barren dusk;
My life is like a frozen thing,
   No bud nor greenness can I see;
Yet rise it shall – the sap of Spring;
   O Jesus, rise in me.

My life is like a broken bowl,
   A broken bowl that cannot hold
One drop of water for my soul
   Or cordial in the searching cold;
Cast in the fire the perished thing;
   Melt and remould it, till it be
A royal cup for Him, my King:
   O Jesus, drink of me.

CHRISTINA ROSSETTI

PARALYTIC

It happens. Will it go on? –
My mind a rock,
No fingers to grip, no tongue,
My god the iron lung

That loves me, pumps
My two
Dust bags in and out,
Will not

Let me relapse
While the day outside glides by like ticker tape.
The night brings violets,
Tapestries of eyes,

Lights,
The soft anonymous
Talkers: 'You all right?'
The starched, inaccessible breast.

Dead egg, I lie
Whole
On a whole world I cannot touch,
At the white, tight

Drum of my sleeping couch
Photographs visit me –
My wife, dead and flat, in 1920 furs,
Mouth full of pearls,

Two girls
As flat as she, who whisper 'We're your daughters.'
The still waters
Wrap my lips,

Eyes, nose and ears,
A clear
Cellophane I cannot crack.
On my bare back

I smile, a buddha, all
Wants, desire
Falling from me like rings
Hugging their lights.

The claw
Of the magnolia,
Drunk on its own scents,
Asks nothing of life.

SYLVIA PLATH

ADDRESS TO MY SOUL

My soul, be not disturbed
By planetary war;
Remain securely orbed
In this contracted star.

Fear not, pathetic flame;
Your sustenance is doubt:
Glassed in translucent dream
They cannot snuff you out.

Wear water, or a mask
Of unapparent cloud;
Be brave and never ask
A more defunctive shroud.

The universal points
Are shrunk into a flower;
Between its delicate joints
Chaos keeps no power.

The pure integral form,
Austere and silver-dark,
Is balanced on the storm
In its predestined arc.

Small as a sphere of rain
It slides along the groove
Whose path is furrowed plain
Among the suns that move.

The shapes of April buds
Outlive the phantom year:
Upon the void at odds
The dewdrop falls severe.

Five-petalled flame, be cold:
Be firm, dissolving star:
Accept the stricter mould
That makes you singular.

ELINOR WYLIE

FLOATING ISLAND AT HAWKSHEAD,
AN INCIDENT IN THE SCHEMES OF NATURE

Harmonious powers with Nature work
On sky, earth, river, lake, and sea:
Sunshine and storm, whirlwind and breeze
All in one duteous task agree.

Once did I see a slip of earth,
By throbbing waves long undermined,
Loosed from its hold; – *how* no one knew
But all might see it float, obedient to the wind.

Might see it, from the verdant shore
Dissevered float upon the lake,
Float, with its crest of trees adorned
On which the warbling birds their pastime take.

Food, shelter, safety there they find
There berries ripen, flowerets bloom;
There insects live their lives – and die:
A peopled *world* it is; – in size a tiny room.

And thus through many seasons' space
This little island may survive
But Nature, though we mark her not,
Will take away – may cease to give.

Perchance when you are wandering forth
Upon some vacant sunny day
Without an object, hope, or fear,
Thither your eyes may turn – the isle is passed away.

Buried beneath the glittering lake!
Its place no longer to be found,
Yet the lost fragments shall remain,
To fertilize some other ground.

DOROTHY WORDSWORTH

The Natural World

OBSERVING and describing the natural world has been a perennial subject for poetry. It may well be poetry's most heavily worked topic, but the range and variety of such poetry seems almost limitless given Nature's own 'infinite variety' and given that every poem is informed by a particular sensibility. In the case of women poets, they are often very sensitively attuned in unexpected ways to the world around them.

A hint of the alienation that we saw in the preceding section seems to appear in the first two poems in this section, by Elinor Wylie and Michael Field (the pseudonym of Katharine Bradley and Edith Cooper). These poets seem to find it impossible to express unalloyed joy at the natural world. Even its manifest beauties and pleasures are tempered by reservations. 'The autumn frosts' and 'Noon' surprise us by the unexpected stings in their tails, so to speak, especially after painting such rich verbal pictures of Nature's luxuriance. Wylie's tribute to her New England climate and landscape, like Field's picture of noon, is Keatsian in its richness. Which of her vignettes of the different seasons' varying gifts do you find most striking or pleasing? Is there beauty in her preferred landscapes or the stark recognition that Michael Field registers? What feeling does the rhythm of her poem convey?

Dorothy Wordsworth starts where Michael Field ends, with sorrow, but moves on to a positive assertion of Nature's personal enrichment. 'Thoughts on My Sick-bed' pays tribute to the power of Nature to revive the human spirit from despondency through the exercise of memory. The poem's spontaneity and childlike joyfulness are quite touching. Dorothy's love of Nature and her communion with it lasted even into old age, and into mental and physical decline. Despite the simplicity of the poem's form, it does not fall into banality, a trap her brother did not always avoid. How does she manage this? Look at her imagery and language. How does she link the inner and outer worlds?

Two poems which share a religious feeling for Nature are the well-known, childlike, lyrical hymn by Mrs Alexander, 'All things bright and beautiful', and 'The Trees Are Down' by Charlotte Mew, with its 'green' sense of apocalypse which is now so topical. Which of the following words would you say describe the tone of these two poems – delight, awe, reverence, wonder? How do they differ?

Emily Dickinson's 'A narrow fellow in the grass', Elinor Wylie's 'Cold-blooded Creatures' and Fleur Adcock's 'For a Five-Year-Old' all look at similarly unlovely and unloved creatures of the natural world. How would you describe the poets' feelings and attitudes towards these creatures – fearful, respectful, sympathetic, indifferent? Emily Dickinson is concerned to give us a vivid description. Look at her language and the order in which she puts her words. Are there any phrases you think particularly striking, and why?

Unlike Emily Dickinson, Wylie and Adcock are less descriptive and more philosophical, finding something to say about human beings generally, or themselves in particular, while still describing their chosen creatures. What is it their poems have to tell us? Which of the two do you find most appealing and why?

The next two poems focus on horses. Sylvia Plath's tremendous description of a horse, 'Whiteness I Remember', is full of life and especially movement, rather like the much more restrained 'A narrow fellow in the grass'. Look at her words and phrases and the way she arranges them. How do they convey the intensity of the experience of being astride a runaway horse? Why is colour important in this poem? Ann Sexton's 'Pain for a Daughter' begins with her child's interest in horses but ends by exploring deeper, more serious issues. What are they? How are they hinted at in the first half of the poem?

Christina Rossetti often disguised her personal feelings behind natural imagery as in 'Another Spring'. What images enable us to infer that this is a poem about love and that the poet recognized she had postponed her pleasures too long and was mistaken in choosing solitariness in place of marriage and children?

The Canadian Elizabeth Brewster's 'Where I Come From', Edna St Vincent Millay's 'Autumn Chant' and Vita Sackville-West's 'Fritillaries' pay tribute to the beauty of Nature. Why might 'Autumn Chant' have appeared in the section on Death? Can you suggest why in both 'Fritillaries' and 'Where I Come From' there is a sense of threat? 'Where I Come From' is a distinctively Canadian poem. What features make it so? Are there any other poems in this anthology that carry with them a similarly pronounced sense of place? This is a good poem to try to imitate in your own writing. Begin, 'Where I come from, people . . .', then go on to say what makes your own locality special and different for you.

From WILD PEACHES

The autumn frosts will lie upon the grass
Like bloom on grapes of purple-brown and gold.
The misted early mornings will be cold;
The little puddles will be roofed with glass.
The sun, which burns from copper into brass,
Melts these at noon, and makes the boys unfold
Their knitted mufflers; full as they can hold,
Fat pockets dribble chestnuts as they pass.

Peaches grow wild, and pigs can live in clover;
A barrel of salted herrings lasts a year;
The spring begins before the winter's over.
By February you may find the skins
Of garter snakes and water moccasins
Dwindled and harsh, dead-white and cloudy-clear.

When April pours the colours of a shell
Upon the hills, when every little creek
Is shot with silver from the Chesapeake
In shoals new-minted by the ocean swell,
When strawberries go begging, and the sleek
Blue plums lie open to the blackbird's beak,
We shall live well – we shall live very well.

The months between the cherries and the peaches
Are brimming cornucopias which spill
Fruits red and purple, sombre-bloomed and black;
Then, down rich fields and frosty river beaches
We'll trample bright persimmons, while you kill
Bronze partridge, speckled quail, and canvasback.

Down to the Puritan marrow of my bones
There's something in this richness that I hate.
I love the look, austere, immaculate,
Of landscapes drawn in pearly monotones.
There's something in my very blood that owns
Bare hills, cold silver on a sky of slate,
A thread of water, churned to milky spate
Streaming through slanted pastures fenced with stones.

I love those skies, thin blue or snowy gray,
Those fields sparse-planted, rendering meagre sheaves;
That spring, briefer than apple-blossom's breath,
Summer, so much too beautiful to stay,
Swift autumn, like a bonfire of leaves,
And sleepy winter, like the sleep of death.

ELINOR WYLIE

NOON

Full summer and at noon; from a waste bed
Convolvulus, musk-mallow, poppies spread
The triumph of the sunshine overhead.

Blue on refulgent ash-trees lies the heat;
It tingles on the hedge-rows; the young wheat
Sleeps, warm in golden verdure, at my feet.

The pale, sweet grasses of the hayfield blink;
The heath-moors, as the bees of honey drink,
Suck the deep bosom of the day. To think

Of all that beauty by the light defined
None shares my vision! Sharply on my mind
Presses the sorrow: fern and flower are blind.

MICHAEL FIELD

THOUGHTS ON MY SICK-BED

And has the remnant of my life
Been pilfered of this sunny spring?
And have its own prelusive sounds
Touched in my heart no echoing string?

Ah! say not so – the hidden life
Couchant within this feeble frame
Hath been enriched by kindred gifts,
That, undesired, unsought-for, came

With joyful heart in youthful days
When fresh each season in its round
I welcomed the earliest celandine
Glittering upon the mossy ground

With busy eyes I pierced the lane
In quest of known and *un*known things,
– The primrose a lamp on its fortress rock,
The silent butterfly spreading its wings,

The violet betrayed by its noiseless breath,
The daffodil dancing in the breeze,
The carolling thrush, on his naked perch,
Towering above the naked trees.

Our cottage-hearth no longer our home,
Companions of Nature were we,
The stirring, the still, the loquacious, the mute –
To all we gave our sympathy.

Yet never in those careless days
When spring-time in rock, field, or bower
Was but a fountain of earthly hope
A promise of fruits and the *splendid* flower.

No! then I never felt a bliss
That might with *that* compare
Which, piercing to my couch of rest,
Came on the vernal air.

When loving friends an offering brought,
The first flowers of the year,
Culled from the precincts of our home,
From nooks to memory dear.

With some sad thoughts the work was done,
Unprompted and unbidden,
But joy it brought to my *hidden* life,
To consciousness no longer hidden.

I felt a power unfelt before,
Controlling weakness, languor, pain;
It bore me to the terrace walk
I trod the hills again; –

No prisoner in this lonely room,
I *saw* the green banks of the Wye,
Recalling thy prophetic words,
Bard, brother, friend from infancy!

No need of motion, or of strength,
Or even the breathing air:
– I thought of Nature's loveliest scenes;
And with memory I was there.

DOROTHY WORDSWORTH

ALL THINGS BRIGHT AND BEAUTIFUL

All things bright and beautiful,
All creatures great and small,
All things wise and wonderful,
The Lord God made them all.

Each little flower that opens,
Each little bird that sings,
He made their glowing colours,
He made their tiny wings.

The purple-headed mountain,
The river running by,
The sunset and the morning,
That brightens up the sky;

The cold wind in the winter,
The pleasant summer sun,
The ripe fruits in the garden –
He made them every one;

The tall trees in the greenwood,
The meadows for our play,
The rushes by the water,
To gather every day; –

He gave us eyes to see them,
And lips that we might tell
How great is God Almighty,
Who has made all things well.

MRS C. F. ALEXANDER

THE TREES ARE DOWN

– and he cried with a loud voice:
Hurt not the earth, neither the sea, nor the trees –
Revelation

They are cutting down the great plane-trees at the end of the gardens.
For days there has been the grate of the saw, the swish of the branches
   as they fall,
The crash of the trunks, the rustle of trodden leaves,
With the 'Whoops' and the 'Whoas,' the loud common talk, the loud
   common laughs of the men, above it all.

I remember one evening of a long past Spring
Turning in at a gate, getting out of a cart, and finding a large dead rat
   in the mud of the drive.
I remember thinking: alive or dead, a rat was a god-forsaken thing,
But at least, in May, that even a rat should be alive.

The week's work here is as good as done. There is just one bough
  On the roped bole, in the fine grey rain,
     Green and high
     And lonely against the sky.
       (Down now! –)
     And but for that,
     If an old dead rat
Did once, for a moment, unmake the Spring, I might never have
  thought of him again.

It is not for a moment the Spring is unmade to-day;
These were great trees, it was in them from root to stem:
When the men with the 'Whoops' and the 'Whoas' have carted the
  whole of the whispering loveliness away
Half the Spring, for me, will have gone with them.

It is going now, and my heart has been struck with the hearts of the
  planes;
Half my life it has beat with these, in the sun, in the rains,
  In the March wind, the May breeze,
In the great gales that came over to them across the roofs from the
  great seas.
  There was only a quiet rain when they were dying;
  They must have heard the sparrows flying,
And the small creeping creatures in the earth where they were lying –
  But I, all day, I heard an angel crying:
  'Hurt not the trees.'

CHARLOTTE MEW

A NARROW FELLOW IN THE GRASS

A narrow fellow in the grass
Occasionally rides;
You may have met him, did you not?
His notice sudden is.

The grass divides as with a comb,
A spotted shaft is seen;
And then it closes at your feet
And opens further on.

He likes a boggy acre,
A floor too cool for corn.
Yet when a child, and barefoot,
I more than once, at morn,

Have passed, I thought, a whip-lash
Unbraiding in the sun,
When, stooping to secure it,
It wrinkled, and was gone.

Several of nature's people
I know, and they know me;
I feel for them a transport
Of cordiality;

But never met this fellow,
Attended or alone,
Without a tighter breathing,
And zero at the bone.

EMILY DICKINSON

FOR A FIVE-YEAR-OLD

A snail is climbing up the window-sill
Into your room, after a night of rain.
You call me in to see, and I explain
That it would be unkind to leave it there:
It might crawl to the floor; we must take care
That no one squashes it. You understand,
And carry it outside, with careful hand,
To eat a daffodil.

I see, then, that a kind of faith prevails:
Your gentleness is moulded still by words
From me, who have trapped mice and shot wild birds,
From me, who drowned your kittens, who betrayed
Your closest relatives, and who purveyed
The harshest kind of truth to many another.
But that is how things are: I am your mother,
And we are kind to snails.

FLEUR ADCOCK

COLD-BLOODED CREATURES

Man, the egregious egoist
(In mystery the twig is bent),
Imagines, by some mental twist,
That he alone is sentient

Of the intolerable load
Which on all living creatures lies,
Nor stoops to pity in the toad
The speechless sorrow of its eyes.

He asks no questions of the snake,
Nor plumbs the phosphorescent gloom
Where lidless fishes, broad awake,
Swim staring at a nightmare doom.

ELINOR WYLIE

WHITENESS I REMEMBER

Whiteness being what I remember
About Sam: whiteness and the great run
He gave me. I've gone nowhere since but
Going's been tame deviation. White,
Not of heraldic stallions: off-white
Of the stable horse whose history's
Humdrum, unexceptionable, his
Tried sobriety hiring him out
To novices and to the timid.
Yet the dapple toning his white down
To safe gray never grayed his temper.

I see him one-tracked, stubborn, white horse,
First horse under me, high as the roofs,
His neat trot pitching my tense poise up,
Unsettling the steady-rooted green
Of country hedgerows and cow pastures
To a giddy jog. Then for ill will
Or to try me he suddenly set
Green grass streaming, houses a river
Of pale fronts, straw thatchings, the hard road
An anvil, hooves four hammers to jolt
Me off into their space of beating,

Stirrups undone, and decorum. And
Wouldn't slow for the hauled reins, his name,
Or shouts of walkers: crossroad traffic
Stalling kerbside at his oncoming,
The world subdued to his run of it.
I hung on his neck. Resoluteness
Simplified me: a rider, riding
Hung out over hazard, over hooves
Loud as earth's bedrock. Almost thrown, not
Thrown: fear, wisdom, at one: all colors
Spinning to still in his own whiteness.

SYLVIA PLATH

PAIN FOR A DAUGHTER

Blind with love, my daughter
has cried nightly for horses,
those long-necked marchers and churners
that she has mastered, any and all,
reigning them in like a circus hand –
the excitable muscles and the ripe neck;
tending this summer, a pony and a foal.
She who is too squeamish to pull
a thorn from the dog's paw,
watched her pony blossom with distemper,
the underside of the jaw swelling
like an enormous grape.
Gritting her teeth with love,
she drained the boil and scoured it
with hydrogen peroxide until pus
ran like milk on the barn floor.

Blind with loss all winter,
in dungarees, a ski jacket and a hard hat,
she visits the neighbours' stable,
our acreage not zoned for barns;
they who own the flaming horses
and the swan-whipped thoroughbred
that she tugs at and cajoles,
thinking it will burn like a furnace
under her small-hipped English seat.

Blind with pain she limps home.
The thoroughbred has stood on her foot.
He rested there like a building.
He grew into her foot until they were one.
The marks of the horseshoe printed
into her flesh, the tips of her toes ripped
off like pieces of leather,
three toenails swirled like shells
and left to float in blood in her riding boot.

Blind with fear, she sits on the toilet,
her foot balanced over the washbasin,
her father, hydrogen peroxide in hand,
performing the rites of the cleansing.
She bites on a towel, sucked in breath,
sucked in and arched against the pain,
her eyes glancing off me where
I stand at the door, eyes locked
on the ceiling, eyes of a stranger,
and then she cries . . .
Oh my God, help me!
Where a child would have cried *Mama!*
Where a child would have believed *Mama!*
she bit the towel and called on God
and I saw her life stretch out . . .
I saw her torn in childbirth,
and I saw her, at that moment,
in her own death and I knew that she knew.

ANNE SEXTON

ANOTHER SPRING

If I might see another Spring,
   I'd not plant summer flowers and wait:
I'd have my crocuses at once,
   My leafless pink mezereons,
My chill-veined snowdrops, choicer yet
   My white or azure violet,
Leaf-nested primrose; anything
   To blow at once, not late.

If I might see another Spring,
   I'd listen to the daylight birds
That build their nests and pair and sing,
   Nor wait for mateless nightingale;
I'd listen to the lusty herds,
   The ewes with lambs as white as snow,
I'd find out music in the hail
   And all the winds that blow.

If I might see another Spring –
   Oh stinging comment on my past
That all my past results in 'if' –
   If I might see another Spring
I'd laugh today, today is brief;
   I would not wait for anything:
I'd use today that cannot last,
   Be glad today and sing.
                CHRISTINA ROSSETTI

AUTUMN CHANT

Now the autumn shudders
  In the rose's root.
Far and wide the ladders
  Lean among the fruit.

Now the autumn clambers
  Up the trellised frame,
And the rose remembers
  The dust from which it came.

Brighter than the blossom
  On the rose's bough
Sits the wizened, orange,
  Bitter berry now;

Beauty never slumbers;
  All is in her name;
But the rose remembers
  The dust from which it came.

EDNA ST VINCENT MILLAY

From THE LAND

So I came through that April England, moist
And green in its lush fields between the willows,
Foaming with cherry in the woods and pale
With clouds of lady's-smock along the hedge,
Until I came to a gate and left the road
For the gentle fields that enticed me, by the farms,
Wandering through the embroidered fields, each one
So like its fellow; wandered through the gaps,
Past the mild cattle knee-deep in the brooks,
And wandered drowsing as the meadows drowsed
Under the pale wide heaven and slow clouds.
And then I came to a field where the springing grass
Was dulled by the hanging cups of fritillaries,
Sullen and foreign-looking, the snaky flower,
Scarfed in dull purple, like Egyptian girls
Camping among the furze, staining the waste

With foreign colour, sulky, dark, and quaint,
Dangerous too, as a girl might sidle up,
An Egyptian girl, with an ancient snaring spell,
Throwing a net, soft round the limbs and heart,
Captivity soft and abhorrent, a close-meshed net,
– See the square web on the murrey flesh of the flower –
Holding her captive close with her bare brown arms,
Close to her little breast beneath the silk,
A gipsy Judith, witch of a ragged tent,
And I shrank from the English field of fritillaries
Before it should be too late, before I forgot
The cherry white in the woods, and the curdled clouds,
And the lapwings crying free above the plough.

VITA SACKVILLE-WEST

WHERE I COME FROM

People are made of places. They carry with them
hints of jungles or mountains, a tropic grace
or the cool eyes of sea-gazers. Atmosphere of cities
how different drops from them, like the smell of smog
or the almost-not-smell of tulips in the spring,
nature tidily plotted in little squares
with a fountain in the centre; museum smell,
art also tidily plotted with a guidebook;
or the smell of work, glue factories maybe,
chromium-plated offices; smell of subways
crowded at rush hours.

           Where I come from, people
carry woods in their minds, acres of pine woods;
blueberry patches in the burned-out bush;
wooden farmhouses, old, in need of paint,
with yards where hens and chickens circle about,
clucking aimlessly; battered schoolhouses
behind which violets grow. Spring and winter
are the mind's chief seasons: ice and the breaking of ice.

A door in the mind blows open, and there blows
a frosty wind from fields of snow.

ELIZABETH BREWSTER

Index of Authors

ADCOCK, Fleur (b. 1934) 167

ALEXANDER, Mrs Cecil Frances
(1818–1895) 164

BARBER, Mary (1690?–1757) 99

BEER, Patricia (b. 1924) 77

BEHN, Aphra (1640–1689) 18

BISHOP, Elizabeth (1911–1979) 72

BLOOM, Valerie (b. 1956) 110

BOWES LYON, Lilian (1895–1949)
90

BRADSTREET, Anne (1612–1672)
22, 55

BREWSTER, Elizabeth (b. 1922) 173

BRONTË, Emily (1818–1848) 14, 58,
71, 87, 137, 151

BROOKS, Gwendolyn (b. 1917) 100

BROWNING, Elizabeth Barrett
(1806–1861) 6, 13, 25, 44, 95

CAVENDISH, Margaret, Duchess of
Newcastle (1624?–1674) 69, 120

CHUDLEIGH, Lady Mary
(1656–1710) 40

COLERIDGE, Mary Elizabeth
(1861–1907) 42, 134, 150

COLLIER, Mary (c. 1689–c. 1762)
103

COLLINS, Anne (c. 1653–?) 56

COPE, Wendy (b. 1945) 139

CORNFORD, Frances (1886–1960)
29, 87

CRAPSEY, Adelaide (1878–1914) 42

DICKINSON, Emily (1830–1886) 47,
61, 64, 70, 78, 140, 166

EGERTON, Sarah Fyge (1669?–1722)
41

ELIOT, George (1819–1880) 48,
116, 133, 152

ELIZABETH I (1533–1603) 8, 151

FANTHORPE, U.A. (b. 1929) 128

FARJEON, Eleanor (1881–1965) 9,
29, 88

FEINSTEIN, Elaine (b. 1930) 22

FIELD, Michael, pseudonym of
Katharine BRADLEY (1846–1914)
and Edith COOPER (1862–1913)
19, 70, 161

FINCH, Anne (1661–1720) 132

GREENWELL, Dora (1821–1882) 115

HERBERT (née Sidney), Mary,
Countess of Pembroke (1561–1621)
55

HOLMES, Pamela (b. 1922) 90

HOOLEY, Teresa (1888–1973) 89

HOWE, Julia Ward (1819–1910) 83

JENNINGS, Elizabeth (b. 1926) 59,
71, 129

LAMB, Mary (1764–1847) 111

LAUGHTON, Freda (b. 1907) 91

LOCHHEAD, Liz (b. 1947) 100

LOWELL, Amy (1874–1925) 147

MAYER, Gerda (b. 1927) 123

MEW, Charlotte (1869–1928) 43, 164

MEYNELL, Alice (1847–1922) 24,
28, 30, 57, 86, 102

MILLAY, Edna St Vincent (1892–1950)
18, 63, 75, 172

MONTAGU, Lady Mary Wortley
(1689–1762) 12

NELSON, Alice Dunbar (1875–1935)
85

NICHOLS, Grace (b. 1950) 74

PHILIPS, Katherine (1632–1664) 24,
146

PICKTHALL, Edith (b. 1893) 91

PLATH, Sylvia (1932–1963) 154, 168

POPE, Jessie (?–1941) 84

RAINE, Kathleen (b. 1908) 23

RICH, Adrienne (b. 1922) 132

RIDLER, Anne (b. 1912) 31, 60, 78

ROSSETTI, Christina (1830–1894) 10,
16, 46, 57, 76, 79, 111, 133, 154, 171

SACKVILLE-WEST, Vita (1892–1962)
130, 172

SCOVELL, E.J. (b. 1907) 31, 32, 51

SEXTON, Anne (1928–1974)   169

SIDNEY, Mary, *see* HERBERT, Mary

SMITH, Stevie (1902–1971)   62

STEVENSON, Anne (b. 1933)   51

WADDINGTON, Miriam (b. 1917)   141

WALKER, Alice (b. 1944)   136

WALKER, Margaret (b. 1915)   152

WARNER, Sylvia Townsend
   (1893–1978)   11, 19, 50, 60, 65

WICKHAM, Anna (1884–1947)   39, 40

WILCOX, Ella Wheeler (1850–1919)
   153

WILKINSON, Anne (1910–1961)   15

WORDSWORTH, Dorothy (1771–1855)
   157, 162

WYLIE, Elinor (1885–1928)   30, 63,
   130, 156, 160, 167

Index of First Lines

A middle-aged farm-labourer lived
   here 90

A narrow fellow in the grass 166

A snail is climbing up the window-
   sill 167

A thousand martyrs I have made 18

Ah! no, not these! 28

Alembics turn to stranger things 130

All craftsmen share a knowledge. They
   have held 130

All things bright and beautiful
   [Mrs C.F. Alexander] 164

All things bright and beautiful [Gerda
   Mayer] 123

All things within this fading world hath
   end 22

And has the remnant of my life 162

Aunt Jennifer's tigers prance across a
   screen 132

Because I could not stop for Death 64

Before she first had smiled or looked
   with calm 32

Belovèd, my Belovèd, when I think 6

Betwixt two *Ridges* of *Plowd-land*, lay
   Wat 120

Blind with love, my daughter 169

Cold in the earth and the deep snow
   piled above thee! 14

Dead! One of them shot by the sea in the
   east 25

Death is the cook of nature and we
   find 69

Do ye hear the children weeping, O my
   brothers 95

Does the road wind uphill all the
   way? 57

Down to me quickly, down! I am such
   dust 70

Drawing you, heavy with sleep to lie
   closer 19

Drowning is not so pitiful 78

Early one morning 60

Fair, do you not see 11

Faith is a fine invention 61

Farewell, you children that I might have
   borne 29

For this your mother sweated in the
   cold 63

Full summer and at noon; from a waste
   bed 161

Harmonious powers with Nature
   work 157

Here is no peace, although the air has
   fainted 63

How simply violent things 87

I a princess, king-descended, decked
    with jewels, gilded, drest 111
I am not human 23
I am the only being whose doom 151
I, being born a woman and distressed 18
I cannot choose but think upon the
    time 48
I dreamt (no 'dream' awake – a dream
    indeed) 57
I gave myself to him 47
I grieve and dare not show my
    discontent 8
I have a friend, a vegetarian seer 116
I have no wit, no words, no tears 154
I heard a fly buzz when I died 70
I love you with my life – 'tis so I love
    you 19
I meant to write a poem upon your
    wedding 51
I sat before my glass one day 150
I saw 89
I saw a boy with eager eye 111
I sing of myself, a sorrowful woman 37
I sit and sew – a useless task it seems 85
I think I was enchanted 140
I thought once how Theocritus had
    sung 6
I told them not to ring the bells 77
I waited ten years in the husk 39
I walk down the garden paths 147
I was a cottage-maiden 10
I wish I could remember that first day 16
I wist not what to wish, yet sure thought
    I 55
If I might see another Spring 171
Illness falls like a cloud upon 31
Immortal Bard! thou fav'rite of the
    Nine! 103
In June and gentle oven 15
In our content, before the autumn
    came 30
In the cold, cold parlour 72
In the daisied lap of summer 141
In the dark and narrow street 115

In the last letter that I had from
    France 88
Is it to me, this sad lamenting strain? 12
It happens. Will it go on? 154
It is to my own as if the man made them
    a gift 145

Kind kettle on my hearth 50

Laugh, and the world laughs with
    you 153
Let them bury your big eyes 75
Lord, on thee my trust is grounded 55
'Love me, for I love you' – and answer
    me 17
Love me, Sweet, with all thou art 44
Love needs not two to render it
    complete 9

Man, the egregious egoist 167
Many in aftertimes will say of you 17
Mine eyes have seen the glory of the
    coming of the Lord 83
Mother, among the dustbins and the
    manure 62
My Dear was a mason 40
My grandmothers were strong 152
My soul, be not disturbed 156

Nature teaches us our tongue again 129
No coward soul is mine 58
No crooked leg, no bleared eye 151
Nothing is lost 78
Now the autumn shudders 172

O may I join the choir invisible 133
O wretch! hath madness cured thy dire
    despair? 99
Oh, once I was a policeman young and
    merry (young and merry) 139
Oh, what a kiss 30
On London fell a clearer light 86
One face looks out from all his
    canvases 133
One wept whose only child was dead 24
Our father works in us 102
Out of the church she followed them 46

People are made of places. They carry
with them 173

Remember me when I am gone away 79

Say, tyrant Custom, why must we
obey 41
School parted us; we never found
again 152
she who has no love for women 22
Silent is the House – all are laid
asleep 137
Since Rose a classic taste possessed 84
So I came through that April England,
moist 172
Such is the force of each created
thing 56

Teach the kings sonne, who king
hymselfe shall be 55
The autumn frosts will lie upon the
grass 160
The child sleeps in the daytime 31
The Church's own detergent 65
The day is done, the winter sun 71
The fat black woman want 74
The first time that the sun rose on thine
oath 7
The slum had been his home since he
was born 91
There is no cross to mark 90
There is no sound of guns here, nor echo
of guns 91
They are cutting down the great plane-
trees at the end of the gardens 164
Thinking of your vocation, I am filled 59
Those dying then 61
Three Summers since I chose a maid 43
Thus rambling we were schooled in
deepest lore 48

'Tis now since I began to die 146
Todder nite mi a watch one
program 110
Twice forty months of wedlock I did
stay 24

We are not dovetailed but opened to each
other 51
We are things of dry hours and the
involuntary plan 100
We had the self-same world enlarged for
each 49
We were first equal Mary and I 100
What is the point 136
When I was a girl by Nilus stream 142
When under Edward or Henry the
English armies 60
When we had reached the bottom of the
hill 9
Where dwell the lovely, wild white
women folk 134
Whiteness being what I remember 168
Why ask to know the date – the
clime? 87
Why were you born when the snow was
falling? 76
Wife and servant are the same 40

'Yes,' I answered you last night 13
You are confronted with yourself. Each
year 71
You are meant to exclaim. The
church 128
You often went to breathe a timeless
air 29
You thought I had the strength of
men 42
You, when your body life shall leave 132

Acknowledgements

The author and publisher wish to thank the following for their permission to reprint material that is in their copyright. Although every effort has been made to contact the owners of the copyright material reproduced in this book, it has not been possible to trace all of them. If we have inadvertently omitted to acknowledge anyone we shall be glad to hear from them so that the appropriate acknowledgements may be included in any future edition.

Fleur Adcock, 'For a Five-Year-Old' from *Selected Poems*, published by Oxford University Press. Reprinted by permission of the publisher.
Patricia Beer, 'Abbey Tomb' from *Collected Poems*, published by Carcanet Press. Reprinted by permission of the publisher.
Wendy Cope, 'A Policeman's Lot' from *Making Cocoa for Kingsley Amis*, published by Faber & Faber. Reprinted by permission of the publisher.
Frances Cornford, 'The Scholar' and 'From a Letter to America on a Visit to Sussex: Spring 1942' from *Collected Poems*, published by Hutchinson. Reprinted by permission of Random House.
Eleanor Farjeon, three sonnets from *First and Second Love*, published by Oxford University Press. Reprinted by permission of David Higham Associates Ltd.
Elizabeth Jennings, 'Rembrandt's Late Self-Portraits', 'To a Friend with a Religious Vocation' and 'A Performance of Henry V at Stratford-upon-Avon' from *Collected Poems*, published by Carcanet Press. Reprinted by permission of David Higham Associates Ltd.
Liz Lochhead, 'The Choosing' from *Dreaming Frankenstein and Collected Poems*, published by Edinburgh University Press. Reprinted by permission of the publisher.
Grace Nichols, 'Tropical Death' from *The Fat Black Woman Poems*, published by Virago. Reprinted by permission of the publisher.
Sylvia Plath, 'Paralytic' from *Ariel* and 'Whiteness I Remember' from *Collected Poems*, edited by Ted Hughes, published by Faber & Faber. Reprinted by permission of the publisher.
Alice Walker, 'Songless' from *Horses Make a Landscape More Beautiful*, published by The Women's Press. Reprinted by permission of David Higham Associates Ltd.
Anne Stevenson, 'An April Epithalamium' from *The Fiction Makers*, published by Oxford University Press. Reprinted by permission of the publisher.
Anne Ridler, 'Nothing Is Lost, 'Now As Then', 'Sick Boy' from *Collected Poems*, published by Carcanet Press. Reprinted by permission of the publisher.
E. J. Scovell, 'Child Waking', 'The First Year', 'Marriage and Death' from *Collected Poems*, published by Carcanet Press. Reprinted by permission of the publisher.
Adrienne Rich, 'Aunt Jennifer's Tigers' from *'The Fact of a Doorframe'. Poems Selected and New, 1950–1984*. Reprinted by permission of the author and W. W. Norton & Company, Inc. Copyright © 1984 by Adrienne Rich. Copyright © 1975, 1978 by W. W. Norton & Company Inc. Copyright © 1981 by Adrienne Rich.